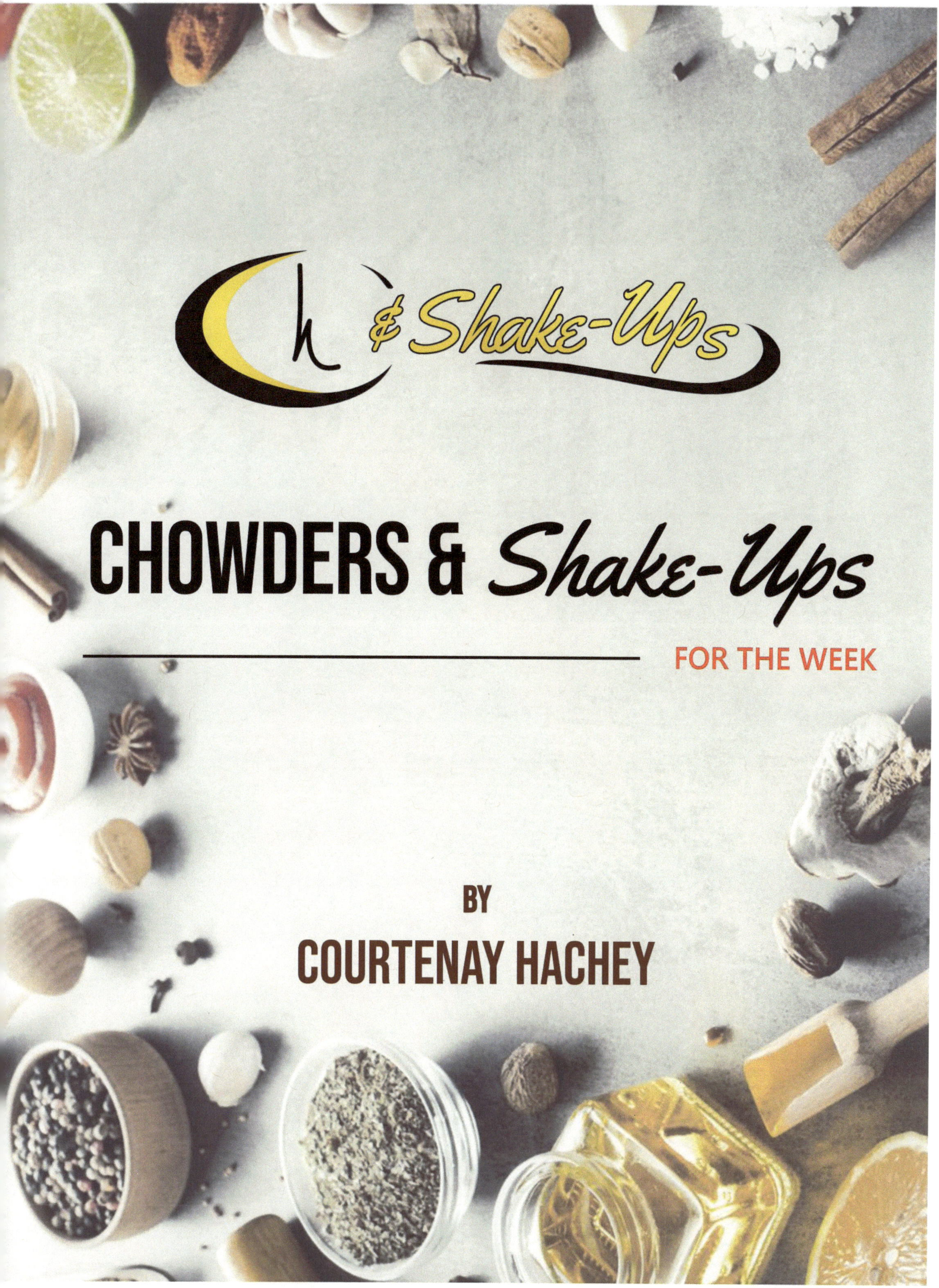

CHOWDERS & *Shake-Ups*

FOR THE WEEK

BY

COURTENAY HACHEY

TABLE OF CONTENTS

TABLE OF CONTENTS

GET READY TO BE

MESMERISED!

INTRODUCTION

My name is Courtenay Hachey of **CHOWDERS &** ***Shake-Ups*** **FOR THE WEEK,** and I am a shameless lover of anything food.

I not only find excitement when experiencing various cuisines, but I also have a passion for creating and writing recipes, and what I call "**Cooking Concepts**".

As for my life journey & how I fell in love with food, it goes back to my younger years.

My parents raised me and my brothers through their Pierogi business in Pennsylvania.

I guess that has always steered me toward food.

This is why, straight out of college, my career began at a restaurant marking firm.

I then spent many tremendous years in the financial industry of New York City.

After some changes happened in my life, I turned to where I am most comfortable and focused solely on cooking and recipe writing.

You see, A passion for Chowders began when I found myself making one every Sunday.

But that's just the beginning.
With that, a "**Cooking Concept**" arrived.
Stick with me - The best is yet to come...

The Novel Concept Is - BOWL TO PLATE Aka Shake-Ups.

I realized that a couple of hours of cooking one Chowder once a week can easily lead to a week's worth of meals.

Give this cooking concept a try. I believe you'll not only enjoy the simple and delicious Chowder recipes,

But you'll have even more fun creating the *Shake-Ups!*

In order to create your first Chowder, the path to success begins with ***JUICY POTATOES.***

You'll find the recipe on Pg. 8 & just about everywhere else in this cookbook.

*CONSIDER THIS COOKBOOK A "**GO-TO GUIDE**" WHEN YOU WANT TO SIMPLIFY YOUR WEEK OF MEALS AND SLOW DOWN ON THE TAKEAWAY.*

CHEERS!

SIMPLE CHOWDER POINTERS – THE CLIFF NOTES:

- Chowders should be made in heavy-bottomed pots – preferably ceramic-covered cast iron – 8 quarts.
- All Chowders (except for vegetarian), start with rendering bacon – and maybe another meat – depending on today's Chowder.
- Remove bacon/meat to a bowl or plate but leave most of the rendered fat/juices in the pot.
- Carrots, Celery, Onions, & Herbs (Fresh Thyme, Rosemary & Bay) are in all Chowders – sautéed in the meat renderings.
- Remove the vegetables to the same bowl as the bacon/meat. Again, keeping the renderings from meat and vegetables in the pot.
- Chopped Potatoes – Russets (creamier) or Yukon's – (heartier) and Onions are in all Chowders to thicken the base – ***JUICY POTATOES (Pg.8).**
- Use Stock (**Homemade – see recipe on Pg. 10**), or good boxed Stock – **NOT** Broth, for the base of all Chowders.
- Stock also helps to loosen the potatoes off the bottom of the pot as they begin to stick when making the **JUICY POTATOES**.
- Meat, Veggies & Herbs are added back to the pot together after the potatoes become tender-crisp.
- Stock is added (3 – 4 Qtrs.) and the Chowder is simmered (with any other ingredients, depending on what type of Chowder you are preparing), for about 45 minutes or until desired thickness.
- Chowders are finished with Heavy Cream or Half & Half – whichever you have on hand or prefer.

DETAILS & INGREDIENTS ARE IN EACH RECIPE – WOULDN'T LEAVE YOU WITHOUT A SOLID ROAD MAP.

DNA/BASE OF CHOWDERS STEP-BY-STEP

INGREDIENTS		STEPS
• 1 lb. of Bacon Veggie lovers (or Vegetarians), simply or frankly, just remove the bacon and you also can **ENJOY CHOWDER**	1	Render your bacon in a ceramic cast iron pot/ Dutch oven on medium-low. Remove when done & chop into bite-size pieces. Remove some of the bacon fat if it seems to be too much for you. Do yourself a favor & leave in at least a couple of tablespoons for flavor.

JUICY POTATOES – Full recipe Page 8

• 3 Large Russet Potatoes • 1 Large or 2 medium Onions • 2 Tbsp. Butter or Olive Oil – or a combination. • 2 Bay leaves • 1 Tbsp. Salt • ½ Tbsp. Pepper • 1 tsp. Thyme – fresh or dried • 1 tsp. Rosemary – fresh • Splashes of Stock or Water – about ¼ - ½ C.	2	I know there is some bacon fat in the pot, but you should add 1 Tbsp. Olive Oil as well. Due to all the starch in potatoes, they will easily stick to the bottom of your pot. Adding splashes of chicken stock while the potatoes & onions cook down, will prevent this as well.
	3	To your pot, on medium-low, add potatoes, onions, herbs, garlic, salt & pepper. ***If you'd like, add 1 - 2 Tbsp. of Butter for flavor. This is optional.*** Splashes of Stock/Water along the way will deliver a similar result. Cook the **JUICY POTATOES** down until the potatoes begin to give off their starch & become tender-crisp. This takes about 10 minutes.

REMAINING DNA:

• 2 medium Carrots • 2 Celery Stocks • 2 Garlic Cloves • ½ C. Half & Half or Heavy Cream	4	When the **JUICY POTATOES** are done, add to the pot, Carrots, Celery, Garlic, your chopped bacon & Stock. Half & Half &/or Heavy Cream comes in at the end. *It's the **FINALE** to all Chowders.*

SERVINGS

- Chowders create 4 to 6 Servings.
- For a family of 4, these Chowder recipes will suffice.
- 1 Chowder dinner and 3 *Shake-Ups*.

** *It's never a bad idea to Double the Chowder Recipes in case your family wants multiple bowls of Chowder on day 1.*

Let's face it, after a long week of work, it's typically pizza & or sandwich night.

When you try this concept of making,
1 Chowder that carries you through the week,
you'll be hooked!

JUICY POTATOES

INGREDIENTS

- 3 Large Russet Potatoes
- 1 Large or 2 small Onions
- 2 Tbsp. Butter - ****Optional***
- 1 Tbsp. Olive Oil
- 1 Tbsp. Salt
- ½ Tbsp. Pepper
- 2 Bay leaves
- 1 tsp. Thyme – fresh or dried
- 1 tsp. Rosemary – fresh or minced
- Splashes of Stock or Water – about ¼ - ½ C.

**** Referring to Step 4*:**
I say optional when it comes to Butter because of 2 Tbsp. Olive Oil along with the splashes of Stock or Water, gets the job done just as well.

STEPS

1
- Begin with 3 large Russet Potatoes to 1 large or 2 small Onions

2
- Chop the onions into a medium dice and chop the potatoes into about ½ in. pieces
- Add 1 Tbsp. Salt ½ Tbsp Pepper to the onions & potatoes.

3
- Sauté them both in a heavy bottomed pot on medium heat with a combination of Olive Oil & Butter (optional).
- For 4 – 6 portions, 2 Tbsp. of butter & 1 Tbsp. Olive Oil is spot on.

4
- Add in your Bay, Rosemary & Thyme. *
- Butter just makes the **JUICY POTATOES** much silkier – **GO FIGURE?**
- Either way, it's all good!

5
- Stir the **JUICY POTATOES** every couple of minutes.
- Be sure to splash in some chicken stock or just water as the onions & potatoes are cooking to keep the starchy potatoes from sticking to the pot.

TIPS

Once the onions are translucent and the potatoes are crisp-tender (not overcooked), they are ready for the base of all your Chowders.

- **Do NOT** take the potatoes to the level of mashed as they will continue to cook in the Chowder.
- We all want a random bite of potato every now & then in Chowders.
- **AND ALWAYS** taste for seasoning. Bland **JUICY POTATOES** are a no-go!
- It should take a total of about **15 minutes** from start to finish.
- Eating this all by itself in a bowl is never a bad idea either.

15 mins

***Economical & comforting*!**

It's worth making on a regular, not just for chowders.
Top the juicy potatoes with a protein of your choice,
(chicken, shrimp, beef, Pork, etc.).

CHICKEN STOCK RECIPE FROM SCRATCH

- If you have the time, make a large batch of chicken stock and freeze whatever you don't use in whichever chowder you are making that week.
- You can always take it out of the freezer and use it in any other dishes you make that week as well. Otherwise, good boxed stock works just as well

PREP TIME 30 mins

COOKING TIME 4 hrs.

INGREDIENTS

- 3 lb. Bone in skinless Chicken Thighs or a 3 lb. Whole Chicken
- 2 large Onions – Yellow or White – quartered – no need to remove skins
- 4 stalks of Celery – cut into large chunks
- 3 Carrots – cut into large chunks
- 1 head of Garlic cut in ½ horizontally to expose the cloves – no need to remove the skin
- 3 or 4 Bay leaves depending on the size of the leaves
- 3 sprigs of Thyme
- 2 sprigs of Rosemary
- 4 Tbsp. of Salt
- 2 Tbsp. of Pepper

TIPS

1 Piece of Parmesan or Pecorino rind from your leftover cheese in the freezer – always keep the rind from your Parmesan cheese for stock.

STEPS

1
- Add all the ingredients (except salt and pepper) into an 8 to 10-quart stock pot with enough water to fully cover the ingredients then bring to a boil.

2
- Once it comes to a boil, add salt & pepper, stir & reduce to a simmer.
- Let it cook with lid ajar for at least **4 hours**.

3
- If Stock forms some foam or fat on top, that's completely normal.

4
- You can skim it off as it is cooking and hot, or you can wait until you refrigerate it for a **few hours** or overnight.
- The foam and fat will somewhat solidify on the top, you can easily scrape it off the top of the stock.

5
- Strain Stock through a colander, remove the chicken & pick the meat off the bones. The chicken is very flavorful due to all the veg & herbs.

***Discard the remaining vegetables and herbs – they did their job.**

HOMEY CHICKEN STOCK DONE – READY FOR CHOWDERS.

TALK ABOUT A GREAT START.

CORN PORK CHOWDER

See Page – 87 For a Recipe.

This photo very well may wet your palate to keep on reading, I certainly hope so!

Chicken Corn Chowder is up next...

If you love sweet corn like
I do try them both.
Two are better than one!

CHICKEN CORN CHOWDER

Believe it or not, the Corn & Pork Chowder photographed on Page 10 & this Chicken Corn Chowder are quite different.
Think Fraternal Twins in Chowder form.

INGREDIENTS

BASE/DNA:

- 1 lb. Bacon
- 2 lb. Chicken Breast – seared in the bacon renderings – or a pulled rotisserie chicken.

JUICY POTATOES:

- 2 large Russet Potatoes
- 1 Large or 2 medium Onions
- 1 tsp. Thyme – fresh or dried
- 1 tsp. Rosemary – fresh
- 2 Bay leaves
- 1 tsp. Salt
- ½ tsp. Pepper

- 3 Small or 2 medium Carrots
- 3 Celery Stocks
- 2 Garlic Cloves
- 6 Fresh Corn cobbs – if it's in season. If not, add ½ lb. of frozen corn.
- 3 – 4 Quarts Chicken Stock – depends on the thickness you want.
- 1 C. Heavy Cream or Half and Half

COOKING TIME 45 mins

STEPS

1

- Begin by searing the bacon on medium in your pot until it's rendered down, but not crispy.
- Remove the bacon onto a paper towel (chop into bite size pieces), until you prepare the chicken – next.

2

- If you are using chicken breast, sear it in the bacon renderings on both sides for a couple of minutes – just to brown it a bit.
- It doesn't need to be completely cooked through as it will finish in the Chowder.

Another good option is to pick up a rotisserie chicken.

- This way, all you must do is pull the chicken off the bone & add it to the Chowder.

THERE'S NO SHAME IN THAT!

3

- Whatever chicken you decide to use, put it on the paper towel with the bacon while you make the **JUICY POTATOES** & sauté the vegetables.
- For chicken breast, chop it into bite-size pieces. As I mentioned above, for rotisserie chicken, just pull it off the bone into whatever size pieces you want in your Chowder.
- See the **JUICY POTATO** ingredients & instructions on **page 8** & everywhere else in this Cookbook for that matter. I can't help myself, it's the core of all Chowders.
- Why use flour when you can thicken your Chowder with **JUICY POTATOES**?

4

- Once the **JUICY POTATOES** are tender-crisp, add in the carrots, celery, corn, stock, reserved bacon & chicken.
- Put the lid on your pot but be sure to keep it ajar.
- The Chowder will take about **45 minutes** to come together & reduce.
- Taste for seasoning & add more salt & pepper if it's calling for it.
- Other than that, just stir in the cream or half & half off the heat so that the dairy doesn't curdle.

BEAUTIFUL CHICKEN CORN CHOWDER –
IT'S TRYING TO HAVE ONLY ONE BOWL.

GO BACK & REFILL UNTIL YOUR TUMMY IS SATISFIED!

TIPS

- If you & your family are cheese fans, top your bowls with grated cheese – You may as well get used to hearing that from me. I tend to squeeze in a bit of cheese if possible. Any gradable cheese in this instance will work.

  In other words, goat or brie doesn't have a place on the top of this chowder – they are too soft.

Nice any time of the year, but especially great in the summer.

Bring it to your friend's Picnic or invite everyone over & have a get-together.

THE CHOWDER WILL BE DONE IN ADVANCE & EVERYONE CAN HELP THEMSELVES.

WHAT FUN!

SWEET CORN & SAVORY CHICKEN.

CHICKEN CORN *Shake-Ups*

CHICKEN CORN PENNE PASTA

CHICKEN CORN MEDITERRANEAN SALAD

CHICKEN CORN PIZZA

Salad, Pasta & Pizza all in ***Shake-Up*** form.

All I have to say is...

CHOWDERS ROCK!

There is a Corn & Pork Chowder in this book as well, but the ***Shake-Ups*** are very different.

Try them both – you'll find it to be well worth it!

Check out the *Shake-Up* photos above and tell me you're not interested.

MEDITERRANEAN SALAD

Yep – Chowder transformed into a salad. What a lovely brunch, lunch or dinner. It's light but still hearty.
A great salad for a group or if you just want a night alone!

STEPS

1
- Warm your Chowder on medium-low in a small saucepan.
- This recipe needs 1 C. Chowder to accommodate 4 salads. Due to all the other ingredients, you don't need that much Chowder.
- Obviously, if you are making 6 salads, just warm another ¼ C.

BEAUTIFUL BOWLED SALAD

2
- After it's warmed, strain it into a bowl using a slotted spoon so you don't have too much liquid.

3
- To the bowled Chowder, add your favorite vinaigrette. I like balsamic vinaigrette, but anything works well with this salad.

If you want to make your own vinaigrette, it's simply 1 part vinegar to 3 parts olive oil, 1 Tbsp. Dijon mustard, 1 tsp. of honey or agave & a pinch of salt & pepper. Whisk it all together & done! You can always use store-bought if you want.

- When dressing the Chowder, start with 3 – 4 Tbsp. You can always add. I find you don't need much dressing with this salad due to all the strong flavors

4
- Tomatoes: You can use any type of tomato you like. I just use whatever looks best in the store.
- Be sure to remove most of the seeds when you are cutting up your tomatoes. They add too much liquid, which will water down your dressing & make your salad too wet. I find 2 large, or 3 smaller tomatoes is a good amount for 4 salads.

You won't believe the flavors… I mean it!
Let's talk olives.

5
- I used Kalamata olives – because I absolutely love them, but you can use any type of dark briny olive you like.
- It depends on which type of olive you choose, but ½ C. cut in half should be enough for 4 salads.

6
- When it comes to onions, typically Mediterranean salads have the addition of sliced red onions. In this case, when I was preparing this salad, I only had white onions on hand so that's what I used.
- The main thing to know when using raw onions is that you **MUST** soak your sliced onions in cold water for at least **5 minutes**. Soaking the onions removes the bite & harshness of the raw onions. What you're left with is a pleasant crunchy mild onion flavor.
- Once you drain the water, dry the onions between paper towels.

YOU CAN MAKE A DISH OF IT AT THIS POINT, BUT WHY NOT BULK IT UP WITH CRISPY GREENS?

7
- The final topping & probably my favorite ingredient in Mediterranean salad is - **FETA!**
- You can use whatever type of Feta you prefer. It comes in different types of milk – cow, sheep & goat. It comes in block form to break into small pieces yourself, or you can get it in a plastic container, already crumbled. I prefer cow & sheep Feta or a combination. It's both salty & creamy – perfect in this type of salad.

In the case of assembling 4 salads, 1 C. of crumbled Feta should be enough.

Hey, I'm not looking, add more if you want!

8
- As for lettuce, which to me, is the most boring component in a Mediterranean salad - I like a combination of Romaine & Iceberg.

A Greek salad is all about the flavorful toppings. In this instance, the lettuce is simply a vehicle to get all that tasty goodness to your mouth.

- Chop the lettuce however large or small you want. I like it right down the middle – not too large or small.
- Put the lettuce in the bottom of your bowls with your dressed Chowder & build the salad however you want as far as the toppings. It's all going to the same place.

Salad is all tossed together so you get many of the delicious ingredients in most bites.

IT'S ALMOST MAGIC

THE SALAD VANISHES IN FRONT OF YOU AS YOU CAN SEE

SALAD & CHOWDER AS ONE. ENJOY THE *Shake-Up!*

CHICKEN CORN PIZZA

TIPS

- For homemade pizzas, I use store-bought dough. All grocery stores have good quality dough, whether that be in the frozen or refrigerated section.
- If you have a local pizzeria, most will sell you a ball of dough on the cheap – not a bad way to go.
- When using frozen dough, take it out of the freezer in the morning on the day you plan to make this pizza.
- By the time you get around to making dinner, the dough will be ready to stretch out & become a nice pizza crust.

STEPS

1

- A very hot oven is crucial when making a crispy yet chewy pizza crust...

Preheat your oven to 450

2

- Before getting to the pizza crust, warm 1 C. of your Chowder in a saucepan on low.
- Par-baked dough prior to topping with warm Chowder & sliced/grated cheese

3

- Before stretching out the dough to fit the pan, coat it with some olive oil – simply coat your hands with a little oil & rub it over the ball of dough. Beyond the flavor it adds, it assists in browning the crust.
- Bring on Chowder pizza ... Strained Chowder layered onto par-baked crust.

4

- Top your pizza with the cheese of your choice.

I chose sliced mozzarella & grated Parmesan.

If you haven't experienced a pizza topped with a Chowder of chicken & corn,

YOU'RE IN FOR A TREAT!

CHICKEN CORN PIZZA – NOT YOUR TYPICAL FRIDAY NIGHT PIZZA DINNER

COME ON, GIVE IT A TRY!

This one has to be wracking your brain.
I mean, Chicken Corn Chowder turned into a pizza?
It's incredible in flavor & easy to throw together.

CHICKEN CORN PENNE PASTA

STEPS

1
- Warm 1 c. Of your chowder in a medium saucepan on low to reduce for a **few minutes – maybe 10**.

2
- As it's warming & reducing, bring a small pot of water to boil for the penne.
- Once the water is boiling, heavily salt it (2 tbsp.) and add your pasta.
- As usual, cook the pasta at least **1 minute** short of the package directions.
- Personally, I think shaving **2 minutes** off is best due to carry-over cooking when the sauce joins the pasta.

CHOWDER REDUCED IN A SKILLET WITH THE ADDITION OF PENNE BEFORE MIXING IT ALL TOGETHER

CHICKEN, CORN, PENNE PASTA DONE. DON'T EVEN TRY TO RESIST IT!

3
- If your pasta & sauce is looking on the thick side, do the following…
- Take some of the **STARCHY, SALTY PASTA WATER** from the pot with a large spoon & add some.
- It will **LOOSEN** the sauce & **PULL THE DISH ALL TOGETHER**.

4
- Top with grated Parm or Pecorino.

Your family will never know that this is the child of a Chowder.

This dish tastes similar to what you would order at an Italian American restaurant.

BUT. MUCH BETTER AND MADE IN YOUR OWN HOME - *SWEET!*

SAUSAGE BROCCOLI CHOWDER

If you've ever lived near or visited Philadelphia or New York City, you've most likely enjoyed a few sausage-broccoli rabe hoagies. Here you have the same flavors, just a different vessel – a bowl instead of a bun

INGREDIENTS

- 1 lb. Bacon
- 1 lb. Italian Sausage – hot, sweet, or a combination of both.

I like spice, so I go with hot, but either is delicious in this dish.

JUICY POTATOES:

- 2 large Russet Potatoes
- 1 Large or 2 medium Onions
- 1 tsp. Thyme – fresh or dried
- 1 tsp. Rosemary – fresh
- 2 Bay leaves
- 1 tsp. Salt
- ½ tsp. Pepper

- 3 Small or 2 medium Carrots
- 3 Celery Stocks
- 2 Garlic Cloves
- 1 head broccoli – cut into small florets
- 2 - 3 Quarts Chicken Stock
- 1 C. Heavy Cream or Half and Half

STEPS

1
- Render down your bacon. Remove it and set it aside to make the sausage.

2
- Sear the sausage in the same pot.
- This will take about **15 minutes** on medium.

3
- Chop the bacon & sausage into bite-size pieces once it's browned & cooked through.

4
- Make the **JUICY POTATOES** in the same pot.

5
- When they're tender-crisp, add the carrots, celery & onions.
- Cook the veggies for **5 minutes** (remember to season with salt & pepper), then return the bacon & sausage back to the pot

6
- Now incorporate the chicken stock. Put a lid ajar on the pot & let simmer on low for **45 minutes**.
- After **45 minutes**, remove the lid & let the Chowder reduce for **15 more minutes** if it hasn't thickened enough.
- Place in the broccoli florets.
- Add half & half or cream off the heat so it doesn't curdle.

TIPS

Feel free to top your bowls of Chowder with some grated cheese, but I think the strong flavors in this Chowder speak for themselves.

SAUSAGE & BROCCOLI CHOWDER PRIOR TO BLUSHING WITH CREAM.

Cheap, easy & beyond delicious!
I think this will become a regular in your home.
It's a great dish for taking to your friend's house as well.

Who needs a roll with sausage & broccoli?

A NICE WARM BOWL IS JUST AS GOOD, IF NOT BETTER!

SAUSAGE BROCCOLI *Shake Ups*

1. Sausage Broccoli Rice Casserole
2. Sausage Broccoli Wrap
3. Sausage Broccoli Bisque Topped with An Egg
4. Bonus - Biscuits & Sausage Chowder Gravy

SAUSAGE BROCCOLI RICE CASSEROLE

The photos below road map this simple *Shake-Up*, but the following will bring it home:

STEPS

1 **Turn your oven to 350 to preheat.**

2 Make 2 C. long grain rice (Jasmine or Basmati), in stock or water according to the package directions.

BUT only cook the rice ½ time in those directions.

Remember, this is a casserole, so the rice is going to continue to cook while it's in the oven.

3 Warm on low 2 C. of your Chowder in a saucepan while the rice is cooking.

Now's the hard part, Kidding of course

WARMING THE CHOWDER

4 Mix the warm Chowder & rice together in a large bowl.

5 Transfer to oven-safe bowls or casserole dish - whichever you prefer.

6 Top the casserole dish with some panko & grated **Parmigiano** or **Pecorino Romano**.

WARMED CHOWDER & CHEESY RICE MIXED IN A GREASED OVEN-SAFE BAKING DISH.

7 Throw it in the oven on the middle rack for **20 minutes**, or until you see it begin to bubble.

Sausage, broccoli, cheese & rice...
No wonder why it's disappearing!

BOOYAH!

FINISHED BAKED CASSEROLE

Look at the golden-brown edges.
Bubbly deliciousness!

SAUSAGE BROCCOLI WRAPS

SAUSAGE, CHICKEN, AND BROCCOLI CHOWDER READY FOR ITS COZY WRAP. A GREAT HAND-TO-MOUTH EASY MEAL.

This Shake-Up is one of those dishes that you make after a long day.

It takes less than **15 mins** from start to finish.

HIGHLIGHTS

1
- Take your Chowder out of the fridge & put it into a saucepan on low to heat through, while you change out of your work clothes.
- This dish only needs 1 ½ C. of Chowder for 4 to 6 portions

2
- Next is to slice some cheese. Grating in this instance doesn't work. The cheese will fall out when you're trying to eat the wrap.
- With that said, a good sliced cheese from your deli counter is perfect for this preparation.

WRAP IT ALL UP AND TAKE A BIG BITE!

STEPS

Speaking of Diving in & Chowing Down…

Here are the specifics of this healthy Wrap recipe

1 Reduce your Chowder (1 C.) down on low in a small saucepan for about **10 minutes**.

2 While that's happening, pull apart some large pieces of crunchy iceberg lettuce – large enough to stuff, wrap & roll.

TIPS

- If you don't have a gas stove, simply put the tortillas under your broiler for a minute on each side – again, until it starts to bubble a bit.
- You can also warm the tortillas on your stovetop in a skillet over high heat for a few seconds on both sides.
- This method works with gas and electricity – no oil is needed.

3

- Now take your flour tortillas and sear them on the top of your stove – if you have a gas stove, that is. Using thongs, flip the tortillas onto the other side after a few seconds – you'll know when it needs to be flipped when it starts to bubble & create golden brown spots.

Any longer than that, they will burn.

4

- Take your seared tortilla to the serving plate and line them with some sliced cheese.
- For this wrap, I like a cheese that isn't too strong in flavor – cheddar, fontina, or gouda is great

5

- Layer some of your reduced Chowder & sturdy greens on top of the cheese as in – Iceberg or Romaine.
- If you would like, top the filling with some salsa & sour cream – OR you can keep those for dipping on the side.
- **Wrap it all up** - Grip it tightly together as you roll them. That way, they will stick together nicely for you.

Look how simple. It's time to assemble...

Once you try this wrap & roll process, there's a good chance it will become a regular in your home.

You can do it with almost any filling.

LET YOUR IMAGINATION EXPLORE

THE POSSIBILITIES!

SAUSAGE BROCCOLI BISQUE

If you're not a fan of sunny-side-up eggs, that's ok, but you're really missing out.

That's ok. I forgive you.

Make an over-light instead. Flip the eggs & you have eggs over-light in less than **30 seconds.**

This is a dish that will inspire you to get imaginative with everyday mundane dinners.

Creativity never hurts, I promise!

WINK

WINK

STEPS

This might sound like a ridiculous *Shake-Up*, but have faith, it absolutely works.

No, that's not correct, it doesn't work, it shines!

Make sure you get home early to make this meal. It's tremendously complex!

1 Using thongs or a spoon for that matter, remove the chopped sausage from the Chowder & package that up for another purpose – or **NOT...***

2 Now pour your **COLD** Chowder into a blender & zap it until it's silky smooth. With this dish, however many servings you are making is how many cups of Chowder you'll need.

****NOTE - It's important that you blend the Chowder when it's cold. If you blend hot food, it can literally blow the lid off & burn you.***

Once the Chowder is at the consistency that pleases you, warm it in a saucepan. This will take, maybe **2 minutes**.

TOAST POINTS FOR DIPPING INTO THE BISQUE & YOLK.

Close Your Eyes & You Might Be Transported to A Parisian Bistro or An Equally Delicious & Charming American New York City Brasserie.

I really, really like a sunny-side-up egg - on almost anything. If you enjoy eggs, I highly suggest that you top this bisque with an egg. The runny yolk is a sauce on its own & you get the benefit of protein from the white of the egg as well.

Speaking of eggs, here is how you make them sunny side up. If you've been unsuccessful in the past, or are just intimidated, stay with me here, this is full proof.

3

- Crack your eggs into a lightly oiled skillet that is barely warm – cold is even ok.
- Turn the heat up to medium-low & don't touch them – other than season with salt & pepper.
- When you see the whites coagulate/turn opaque, put the pan of eggs, under your broiler for exactly 2 minutes. Make sure that you are using a pan that is safe to use in the oven.

Look at that. Eggs are done, Chowder is warm & it's time to eat.

TIPS

- **Note: *If you chose to remove the sausage from the Chowder prior to pureeing it, think breakfast...**

Sausage in your scrambled eggs - Sausage cheese toast or sandwich. - Sausage on top of your oatmeal or grits, etc.
The tasty possibilities are endless.

Full disclosure – I leave in the sausage.

Once it's all blended, the finished bisque is much smoother than you would believe!

Decadent is the word that comes to mind. More importantly, decadence is what lands in your bowl.

THAT'S ONE SWIFT
HEALTHFUL DINNER!

BONUS - BISCUITS & SAUSAGE GRAVY

QUICK & SIMPLE DROP BISCUITS

CHECK OUT THE DETAILS

STEPS

If you grew up on Biscuits & Gravy, this dish will provide a nice twist on the traditional B&G.

1

- Begin by warming your Sausage Chi Chowder (1 C.) in a small saucepan on low until warmed through – **5 – 7 minutes**.
- You **DON'T** need to cook the Chowder down much in this recipe as it's going to play as the gravy.

You & your family are meat eaters. Another seared piece of sausage won't hurt this dish. Another piece of sausage wouldn't hurt should your family be meat-eaters.

2

- Just sear the pork, turkey, or chicken link in a nonstick pan with a drizzle of olive oil and a couple of splashes of chicken stock. Cover the pan with a lid or a piece of foil and sear for about **3 minutes** on each side.

Remember that the sausage is going to be added to the warmed Chowder, so if it's not completely cooked through, it will finish cooking in the Chowder gravy.

3

- Once the sausage has rested for **5 minutes**, cut it up into small bite-size pieces and add it to your warmed Chowder gravy.

Note: You can also use bulk sausage if your store carries it. I know it's popular to use breakfast sausage in Biscuits & Gravy. If that's your preference & tradition, add some (¼ lb.) to the warm Chowder. Keep it on low until the biscuits are done baking

Speaking of biscuits, let's make some.

START MAKING DROP BISCUITS WITH VERY COLD BUTTER INTO YOUR DRY MIXTURE.

4

Drop biscuits are awesome. There is no reason for rolling them out. Scrap the countertop mess with all that flour.

Preheat your oven to 400.

5

In a large bowl, add the following:

- 3 C. All-purpose flour
- 2 Tsp. baking powder
- 1/8th tsp. salt – basically a good pinch
- 1 ½ sticks of **VERY COLD** butter, cut into small pieces

6
- Mix together the dry ingredients & then add the cold butter.

If you have one, you can use a pastry cutter to combine the butter with the dry ingredients. Otherwise, two butter knives do the job of breaking up the cold butter into the flour mixture until it resembles small peas.

- A food processor is nice for this type of dough as well. I just don't like cleaning it – call me lazy.
- If you do use a food processor, make sure you only pulse the butter into the dry mixture. The blade of the processor gets warm as it works & can start to melt the butter. No matter what preparation you go with, don't over-mix.

7
- To finish the batter, add 1 ¾ C. buttermilk. You can also use whole plain milk if you desire, but I like the tang of buttermilk – again, please don't over-mix.

8
- Foil & butter your baking sheet

9
- Drop dollops of the biscuit batter onto the buttered baking sheet about ½ in. apart.

10
- Bake on the middle rack of your oven until golden brown on top – it should take **12 - 15 minutes**.

TIPS

You can brush the biscuits with some melted butter for extra flavor after you take them out of the oven – if your heart desires.

I know mine does

SAUSAGE BROCCOLI CHOWDER GRAVY OVER BISCUITS – *NICE!*

CHEESEBURGER CHOWDER

What do you order on Cheeseburgers?
GO FOR IT. Nothing is out of bounds!

INGREDIENTS

LETS GET THE BASE/DNA GOING FIRST:

- 1 lb. Bacon
- 1.25 lb. Ground Beef – I prefer 80/20

JUICY POTATOES

- 2 Russet Potatoes - chopped
- 1 Large or 2 medium Onions – chopped
- 2 - 3 Tbsp. Butter added to the potatoes for flavor
- That's your call. It's not critical, but it does make a delicious difference.
- 1 tsp. Thyme – fresh or dried
- 1 tsp. Rosemary – fresh
- 2 Bay leaves
- 1 tsp. Salt
- ½ tsp. Pepper

REMAINING INGREDIENTS

- 3 Small or 2 medium Carrots - chopped
- 3 Celery Stocks - chopped
- 2 Garlic Cloves – minced/finely chopped
- 2 - 3 Quarts Chicken Stock
- 1 C. Heavy Cream or Half and Half
- ¼ lb. Grated Cheddar Cheese

TIPS

For topping the bowls of Chowder when serving:

- Chopped fresh Tomatoes, raw Onion (green or white), shredded Lettuce, pickles, or whatever fresh toppings you enjoy on your burgers.

As you can see pictured above, I'm pickle obsessed.

STEPS

1

- As with all Chowders, begin by sautéing the bacon in your cast iron or heavy-bottomed pot.
- When the bacon has rendered out most of its fat, remove it using thongs and place it on paper towels.
- Chop the bacon into bite-size pieces.

2

- Now, take your beef & add it to the pot with the bacon renderings. If you think there is too much fat in the pot, feel free to spoon out some of it.
- With that said, I highly recommend keeping at least a couple Tbsp., both for flavor & as a non-stick agent.
- Using a plastic spatula or spoon, break up the meat on medium-low until it's golden brown and cooked through.

3 Once the meat is done, remove it from the pot & put it aside – just as you did with the bacon. Set aside until the **JUICY POTATOES** are complete.

Speaking of that, JUICY POTATOES – here we go.

4
- I know there is some bacon & beef fat in the pot, but add 1 Tbsp. Olive oil as well. Trust me!
- Due to all the starch in potatoes, they will easily stick to the bottom of your pot.
- Adding splashes of chicken stock while the potatoes & onions cook down will prevent sticking as well.
- Add potatoes, onions, herbs, garlic, salt & pepper to your pot on medium-low heat

If you'd like, add a couple Tbsp. of butter for flavor. This is optional. **See exacts – Page 8**

5
- Cook the **JUICY POTATOES** down until the potatoes begin to give off their starch & are tender-crisp. This takes about **10 – 15 minutes**.

***We're not looking for mashed potatoes - they will continue to cook once all the ingredients are together in the pot.**

- Remember to remove the bay leaves & thyme sprigs before adding everything else to the pot.

6
- To the creamy, silky **JUICY POTATOES**, it's time to dump all the goodness into the pot:
- Bacon, browned ground meat, carrots, celery – season with salt & pepper & add the stock.

NOTE – Seasoning with salt & pepper every time you add an ingredient will result in a much tastier & well-rounded flavor.

7
- Put a lid onto the pot (ajar) and cook on medium-low for approximately **45 minutes** to an hour.
- Check to be sure that it's not bubbling too much. You're looking for a light simmer. If it bubbles too much, you can easily burn yourself & also make a mess of your stove.

8
- After **45 minutes**, taste for seasoning & texture. If it's still on the thin side, take the lid off and cook for another **10 - 15 minutes**.

9
- Off the heat, and finish by stirring in your half & half or heavy cream & grated cheese.

You Can Always Top the Chowder with Some More Grated Cheese If You Want, Even Though There Is Plenty Inside the Chowder.

I'm Cheesy, Are You?

CHEESEBURGER IN A BOWL

BRING ON CHEESEBURGER NIGHT!

CHEESEBURGER *Shake Ups*

1. Cheeseburger Bolognese
2. Cheeseburger Queso
3. Cheeseburger Stacked Salad

CHEESEBURGER BOLOGNESE

HERE SHE IS... CHEESEBURGER BOLOGNESE

In all reality, this isn't exactly Bolognese, but it's a great quick fake on a dish that takes up to 4 – 6 hours. This one can be finished in 20 minutes or less with the help from all the flavors in the Chowder – YEP!

STEPS

THIS SHAKE-UP ISN'T ANY DIFFERENT THAN THE REST... IT'S REDICULOUSLY SIMPLE!

1. Bring a pot of water to boil for your pasta.
2. Reduce 2 C. Cheeseburger Chowder in a medium saucepan.
3. When the Chowder has condensed (about **5 – 7 mins**), add in 1 C. *Red Wine & simmer on low for **3 – 5 minutes** or until it's thick enough to coat your pasta.
   Speaking of that, drop your pasta. Be sure to heavily salt the pasta water once it comes to a boil. Cook it to package directions – minus **1 min**.
4. After draining your pasta, mix it with the reduced Chowder and top with some grated Parm or Pecorino & that's all she wrote.

TIPS

*Any dry red you like to drink - Cabernet, Merlot, Syrah, etc.

CHEESEBURGER QUESO

FROM A BOX ON THE GROCERY STORE SHELF... HECK NO!
This is meaty, cheesy, hearty, **QUESO!**
Bulk it up with Pasta & you have a stovetop Burger with Mac & Cheese.

STEPS

COMMENCE THE PARTY FOOD OR SIMPLY HAPPY FOOD!

1

- Spoon about 1 C. of your Cheeseburger Chowder into a medium saucepan & warm on low to reduce a little. It will take approximately **10 minutes.**

With this recipe, you definitely don't want to warm it on high heat – only low, or you'll end up with cheese seizing and sticking to the bottom of the pan.
This IS NOT your typical Queso – or at least what most think of Queso. I think.
You know what I'm talking about – the block of processed cheese melted together with a can of tomatoes and some chilis & onions in it.
This is a WHOLE different flavor and texture, but a darn good one!

2

Once your Chowder is warmed through & reduced, add the following to the saucepan:

- 1 C. Shredded white Cheddar cheese
- ¼ C. of your favorite salsa or your homemade Pico de Gallo. And folks, that's pretty much all she wrote.
- Mix the cheese & salsa into the Chowder until the cheese begins to melt.

As I mentioned, this Queso will be on the stringy cheese pull side, not the milky side. Once you test it with a chip or even a spoon & the cheese is pulling away, you're done.

- Top the meaty cheesy Queso with some cilantro and or some chopped scallions and there you have it.

TIPS

- To stretch your Queso Shake-Up even further, just boil 1 lb. pasta of your choice, mix it with warm Queso in a pot & you have a meaty stove-top Mac & Cheese.

Speaking of stretching, you might need to after hammering down this one!

THE ULTIMATE SHAKE-UP:
Chowder, Burger, Queso & Mac & Cheese!

CHEESEBURGER STACKED SALAD

Here's another SHAKE-UP where the Chowder doesn't need to be warmed.

In fact, this dish doesn't include cooking at all.

It's a modest layered salad

Don't let your eyes deceive you. It's WAY heartier than it looks.

My husband & I only ate half for dinner & we were both satisfied.

The Chowder & cheese is the kicker that takes it over the top.

Now onto the layering process: Relax, this process is complex – as complicated as tying your shoes, maybe?

Cheeseburger Chowder stacked with Iceberg lettuce & Provolone cheese.... Huh?

STEPS

1. Using a glass bowl **(approximately 2 Qtrs. For 4 – 6 people)**, spoon in a thin layer **(½ C.)** of the cold Chowder on the bottom of the bowl.

2. Top the Chowder with Iceberg lettuce – a thick layer **(1 in.)**.

   You want the thick layer of lettuce to hang tough/remain crispy while it is resting/compressing in the fridge.

3. Add another layer of Chowder onto the lettuce.

4

- Cover the top entirely with your sliced Provolone.
- Repeat the layering – Chowder, Lettuce, Cheese.

A few more instructions/tips are up next.

Now that the layers of Chowder, lettuce & cheese are stacked, it's time to put some weight on the salad to help it all become one.

5

- I like topping the salad with foil first & then putting a large can of tomatoes, soup or whatever you have lying around, on the foil – hence the photos.
- Nothing left to do here other than wait about **30 minutes** while the salad comes together in the fridge.

ALL THE LAYERS WILL MAGICALLY BECOME ONE AFTER REFRIGERATING.
Think sweet trifle in a savory salad format.
Get it? Hey, give me credit for trying

6

- Using a big plastic or metal spoon, loosen the salad out of the bowl onto a large plate. Shockingly, it will slide right out and stay intact.

7

- Slice it into quarters for a nice brunch, lunch or dinner.
- Another option is slicing it into eights (for a delicious bite at a cocktail party).
- Use toothpicks to keep the salad bites together.

I highly suggest that you try this. It is such a unique salad presentation.

Your family & or guests will be impressed – not just by the look but also by the robust flavors.

WEIGHTING THE SALAD

YOU'LL NEVER THINK OF SALAD

THE SAME WAY AGAIN!

STEAKHOUSE CHOWDER

WHO DOESN'T ORDER A JUICY STEAK & A SIDE OF CREAMED SPINACH WHEN VISITING A STEAKHOUSE?

INGREDIENTS

BASE/DNA

- 1 lb. Bacon
- 1 lb. Hanger, Flank or Flatiron Steak

JUICY POTATOES

- 2 large Russet Potatoes
- 1 Large or 2 medium Onions
- 1 tsp. Thyme – fresh or dried
- 1 tsp. Rosemary – fresh
- 2 Bay leaves
- 1 tsp. Salt
- ½ tsp. Pepper

To the JUICY POTATOES:

- 3 Small or 2 medium Carrots
- 3 Celery Stocks, both chopped
- 2 Garlic Cloves - minced
- 1 16oz. bag frozen chopped Spinach
- 1 block / 8 oz. Cream Cheese
- ½ tsp. Cayenne Pepper
- 2 Quarts Chicken Stock, Homemade or boxed – not broth
- 1 C. Heavy Cream or Half and Half

STEPS

1

- Take your frozen spinach out of the freezer. Open it, place it in a bowl or on some paper towels to begin defrosting.
- In the time it takes to prepare the rest of the Chowder, the spinach should be defrosted enough to squeeze out the extra water.
- It is extremely important that you put the spinach in a dish towel or some cheese cloth - twist it together and squeeze out all the water – the dryer, the better.

YOU DON'T WANT WATERED DOWN CHOWDER

2

- As with all Chowders, begin by sautéing the bacon in your cast iron or heavy-bottomed pot.
- When the bacon has rendered most of its fat, remove it using thongs and place it on paper towels.
- Chop into pieces once it has cooled off.

3

- As the bacon is rendering, slice your steak thinly **across the grain.**

***If you check out the photos, the grain is running horizontally, which means you need to cut it vertically.**

4

- Aggressively season your sliced steak with salt & pepper & add it (in small portions) to the pot with the bacon renderings.
- If you think there is too much fat in the pot, feel free to spoon some of it out.
- With that said, I highly recommend keeping at least a couple Tbsp., both for flavor & as a non-stick agent.

SLICED STEAK – ACROSS THE GRAIN
DEFROSTED DRAINED SPINACH

5

- Sear/sauté the steak on medium-high (using thongs) until it's golden brown and cooked through.

NOTE: Don't overcrowd the pot with the sliced steak. You want to sear/sauté the steak – brown it.

- If you overcrowd the pot, it will steam (turn grey) instead of browning. Because the steak is thinly cut, browning will only take **2 – 3 minutes**.

6

- Once the meat is done, using your thongs, remove it from the pot & put it on a large cutting board or plate.
- Set aside until they are complete – see below

7

- After the steak has rested for about **3 – 5 minutes**, chop it into bite-size pieces.

Think - what size of steak will easily fit on your spoon with everything else in the Chowder.

JUICY POTATOES – in the house!

8

- I know there is some bacon fat in the pot, but you should add 1 Tbsp. Olive oil in the pot as well.
- Due to all the starch in potatoes, they will easily stick to the bottom of your pot.
- Adding splashes of chicken stock while the potatoes & onions cook down will prevent this as well.

9

- To your pot, add potatoes, onions, herbs, garlic, salt & pepper on medium-low heat. See the exact amounts– **Page 8.**
- If you'd like, add a couple Tbsp. of butter for flavor. This is optional.
- Cook the **JUICY POTATOES** down until the potatoes begin to give off their starch & are tender-crisp. This takes about **10 minutes**.

Time to dump everything else into the pot:

10

- Bacon, steak, drained, chopped spinach, carrots, celery – season with salt & pepper & add stock.

NOTE – Seasoning with salt & pepper every time you add an ingredient will result in a much tastier & well-rounded flavor.

11

- Put a lid onto the pot (ajar) and cook on medium-low for approximately **45 minutes** to an hour.
- Check to be sure that it's not bubbling too much. You're looking for a light simmer.
- Taste for seasoning & texture. If it's still on the thin side, take the lid off and cook for another **10 – 15 minutes**.

12 - Off the heat, finish with your room temperature cream cheese & half & half or heavy cream.
- Taste it again for seasoning & add a dash of cayenne if you would like.

CLOSE YOUR EYES, AND YOU'RE AT A STEAKHOUSE WITHOUT YOUR BANK ACCOUNT TAKING A HIT!

STEAKHOUSE *Shake Ups*

1. *Steakhouse Burrito/Wraps*
2. *Steakhouse Mac & Cheese*
3. *Steakhouse Quesadillas*
4. *Bonus! - Steakhouse Nachos*

STEAKHOUSE WRAPS

WRAPS THAT ARE NOTHING SHORT OF LUXURIOUS!

OTHER THAN MAKING SOME EXTRA SEARED ONIONS & OR BELL PEPPERS IN A SKILLET, THE CHOWDER DOES THE WORK FOR YOU.

STEPS

TAKE A BIG BITE. DON'T BE SHY.
YOU WON'T REGRET IT!

GET YOUR NAPKINS READY!

1
- Warm 2 C. of Chowder in a small saucepan or skillet on low.

2
- If you would like sliced seared onions & or bell peppers (as I do), in a separate skillet, with 1 TBSP. of olive oil, cook them on medium-low for 5 minutes.

3
- Add a few splashes of stock or even water if the onions begin to blacken. You're only looking for a light golden color on the onions - you still want them to add some texture to the wrap.

I don't know about you, but soft tortilla wraps call for some crunch inside.

4
- Put your flour tortillas on a glass plate, in the microwave covered with moist paper towels or kitchen towels (bottom & top), for **30 seconds** - or go with the package directions.

If you don't, the wraps will not roll as easily & may break. The Chowder & (if you choose to use), extra grated cheese, will glue it together perfectly.

- Mix together the warm Chowder, sautéed onions & top with grated cheese of your choice.
- Wrap & roll these babies & you're done!

STEAKHOUSE SPINACH MAC & CHEESE

YOU'LL FIND THAT THIS SHAKE-UP COMES TOGETHER EVEN EASIER THAN THE GROCERY STORE BOXED VERSION.

STEAK, SPINACH, PASTA & CHEESE... THAT'S ALL I HAVE TO SAY!

NOT TO MENTION HOW MUCH MORE FLAVOR IT BRINGS TO YOUR DINNER TABLE!

STEPS

1

- Begin by grating 2 C. of Monterey jack cheese or pepper jack cheese (if you like a little spice).
- A good cheddar also is a nice choice. Set it aside.

2

- Warm the Chowder (1 ½ C.) in a saucepan on low.
- If it begins to bubble too much, turn it off.
- Between the warmth of the pasta, Chowder & cheese, all will come together nicely to make a ridiculous stovetop...

MAC & CHEESE

3

- Once the Chowder is warm, mix in the grated cheese until it's melty & coagulated.
- It should look similar to Queso.
- Turn the heat down to LOW, put a lid or some foil on the cheesy Chowder until the pasta is done – which is next.

REDUCING CHOWDER

PASTA

4

- Using a good size pot, fill it halfway with water & bring to a boil.
- For this meal, I used old school elbows, but you can use any kind of short pasta you like.
- Typically, I preach salting the water so that it tastes like the sea, but in this case, the Chowder & cheese brings plenty of salt to the dish so you can skip that step – or just add a little (good pinch) salt to the water.

5

- As always with pasta, boil it **1 to 2 minutes** shorter than the package directions.
- The sauce will continue to cook the pasta as you combine it all together – **No mushy pasta here, please – or EVER!**

Try to contain yourself for the challenging finish

- Drain the pasta, pour it into the pot of Chowder cheesiness & stir together.

WHEW! THAT'S ONE ROUGH SHAKE-UP!

STEAKHOUSE CHOWDER NACHOS

STEPS

NACHOS!

1 Reduce your Chowder (1 ½ C.) on medium-low for about 10 minutes or until you are happy with the thickness.

2 Make your own tortilla chips by baking fresh corn tortillas from the refrigerated section of your grocery store in a 400 oven for 6 minutes.

Lay tortillas (oiled & salted) on a large sheet pan lined with foil.

I like to brush a tiny bit of oil (Olive, Sunflower, Safflower, etc.) on both sides of the tortillas & sprinkle with a little salt for extra flavor.

NOTE – Or make your own by buying them out of a bag from your local store – wink wink!

When it comes to topping the nachos, I prefer a few layers.

PLEASE DON'T JUST PUT A PILE OF CHIPS DOWN AND THEN TOP WITH ALL THE GOOD STUFF.

When using bagged chips, you need to make at least a couple layers so all the chips are covered and yummy.

Think of it as the way you build lasagna.

3 Put grated or sliced cheese onto the tortillas first so the chips don't get soggy.

4 After the cheese, drizzle on your reduced Chowder and then add another thin layer of cheese.

Do the same routine for however many layers you are making.

BEAUTIFULLY TOASTED TORTILLA WITH THE FIRST LAYER OF CHEESE.

I Used Cheddar but Use Whatever You Want. There's No Wrong Turn in This Recipe.

Reduced Chowder on Cheesy, Crisped Tortilla Then Another Layer of Cheese on Top

5

- Put Nachos back into the 400 oven for **10 minutes** or until you see the cheese is melted.
- As for the extra good stuff – NACHO TOPPINGS, I think Pico de Gallo/salsa, sour cream & chopped avocado tastes great.

On the right, is what the tortilla looks like when it comes out of the oven.
Both layers of cheese have melted & are one with the warm reduced Chowder.

This might be fast, but it's certainly

NOT FAST FOOD!

IT IS HOWEVER, A FANTASTIC

SHAKE-UP!

Tortilla cut into Nachos.
No need for utensils.
Pick them up!

CRUNCHY, CHEESY, CREAMY & SPICY (FROM THE PICO).

DON'T WAIT FOR A GAME TO MAKE

NACHOS!

STEAKHOUSE QUESADILLAS

FOLLOW THIS PATH TO QUESADILLAS...

When I said these are decadent, I meant it.
The Chowder itself is so luxurious, it doesn't take much to turn it into a wonderful Quesadilla.

STEPS

Here's how you do it.

1
- Warm your Chowder in a small saucepan. Two C. will be plenty for 4 large Quesadillas.
- Once you cut the quesadillas into 4 triangular segments (as you would see in any restaurant), the result is 16 pieces.

2
- When the Chowder is warmed through, add approximately 1 C. of shredded cheese.
- For Quesadillas, my preference is Pepper Jack, but you can use Monterey Jack, or Sharp Cheddar if you don't enjoy spice. Guess what, we're pretty much there.

Let's talk flour tortillas.

3
- Warm the flour tortillas over an open flame for 5 seconds a side. Use thongs to turn them so you don't burn yourself. Or for an electric stove, put them in a hot, dry skillet and warm the tortillas that way.
- It takes about a minute a side to warm & turn pliable.
- To ERR on the side of caution, just soften them in the microwave for 10 seconds between moistened paper towels.

I already can see the goal line!

4
- Spoon some of the cheesy steaky Chowder mixture onto one of the warm tortillas, sprinkle on the grated cheese & top with another tortilla to finish.
- Give them **2 minutes** to rest so the cheese doesn't ooze out too much, but after that...

GO FOR IT!

5 Top with crema (sour cream mixed with a drizzle of lime juice & a pinch salt & pepper), Pico d' Gallo (recipe below), or your favorite **STORE-BOUGHT** salsa if you'd like.

STUFFED QUESADILLA TOPPED WITH CREMA & PICO D' GALLO

Grab your knife & fork for this decadent Quesadilla!

WHAT A BEAUTY!

PICO D' GALLO

INGREDIENTS

- 3 Roma or vine ripened tomatoes
- 1 small or half medium white onion
- 1 Jalapeno pepper or serrano if you like it spicy.
- Juice of one lime
- Salt & Pepper – couple pinches
- Chopped or ripped cilantro if you'd like.

STEPS

1 Chop the onion into a tiny dice & let it rest in a bowl of cold water for **5 minutes** – cold water takes the sting out of onions.

2 If you have a food Processor, making Pico de Gallo takes minutes.

3 You can chop the veg into large pieces & the Pro does the rest of the work.

DON'T SWEAT IT IF YOU DON'T HAVE THE EQUIPMENT.
USE YOUR FAVORITE STORE-BOUGHT SALSA.

WITH THAT SAID, TREAD LIGHTLY WITH HOMEMADE PICO, IT'S BEYOND ADDICTING.

I PUT IT ON ALMOST EVERYTHING!

CHICKEN MUSHROOM CHEESESTEAK CHOWDER

If you're into Chicken Cheesesteaks instead of beef, this recipe is right up your alley. Should mushrooms not be for you, omit them & add additional chicken.

ITS AWESOME EITHER WAY!

INGREDIENTS

- 1 lb. Bacon
- 1 Rotisserie Chicken (approximately 3 lbs.) pulled off the bone into bite-size pieces. Use the skin if you want, but I think is better without. It tends to get gummy in the Chowder.

Remember, you have the fat from the bacon

JUICY POTATOES

- 2 large Russet Potatoes – ¼ in. slices
- 1 Large or 2 medium Onions – medium dice
- 1 tsp. Thyme – fresh or dried
- 1 tsp. Rosemary – fresh – finely diced
- 2 Bay leaves
- 1 Tbsp. Salt
- ½ Tbsp. Pepper

REMAINING INGREDIENTS

- 3 Small or 2 medium Carrots
- 3 Celery Stocks
- 2 Garlic Cloves
- 8 oz. Package of Mushrooms
- Baby Bellas or White Button Mushrooms – Sliced thickly.
- 2 Quarts Chicken Stock
- 1 C. Grated Cheddar
- 6 oz. Cream Cheese
- 1 C. Heavy Cream or Half and Half
- Top your bowls with grated provolone or cheddar cheese when serving

STEPS

1

- Render your bacon in the pot on medium low. Remove when done to paper towels & chop into bite size pieces.

2

- Once the Bacon has rendered, sear the mushrooms in the bacon fat until they begin to brown.
- Remove some of the bacon fat if it seems to be too much for you.
- Do yourself a favor & leave in at least a couple tablespoons for flavor.
- When you see the mushrooms turn golden brown remove from the pot with a slotted spoon and let rest with the bacon.

3

- I know there is some bacon fat in the pot, but you should add 1 Tbsp. olive oil as well.
- Due to all the starch in potatoes, they will easily stick to the bottom of your pot.
- Adding splashes of chicken stock while the potatoes & onions cook down will prevent this as well.

4

- To your pot, on medium-low heat, add potatoes, onions, herbs, garlic, salt & pepper.

See INGREDIENTS for exact amounts. If you'd like, add a couple of Tbsp. of butter for flavor. This is optional.

- Cook the **JUICY POTATOES** down until the potatoes begin to give off their starch & become tender-crisp. This takes about 10 minutes.

GRAB A SPOON. CHEESESTEAK IN A BOWL, IS UP!

5
- When the **JUICY POTATOES** are done, add to the pot, all the veg, bacon, pulled chicken, mushrooms & stock.
- Cook the Chowder on medium-low with a slanted lid or at least a piece of foil, so it doesn't reduce too much.
- It should take only about **45 minutes** until it's done and ready for the cheese & cream.

6
- Taste for seasoning & add more salt & pepper if it's calling for it.
- Once it tastes like the greatest chicken mushroom soup you ever had, add the cheese & cream – be sure the pot is off the heat when you add dairy so it doesn't separate.

If you want, top the bowls with some more grated cheese. I did!

THAT'S IT - CHICKEN CHEESESTEAK MUSHROOM CHOWDER

YOU'LL LIKE IT MORE THAN A CHICKEN MUSHROOM CHEESESTEAK.

OK, MAYBE JUST AS MUCH!

CHICKEN MUSHROOM CHEESESTEAK *Shake Ups*

1. *Chicken Mushroom Ramen*

2. *Chicken Mushroom Quesadilla*

3. *Chicken Mushroom Burrito*

4. *Chicken Mushroom Skillet*

CHICKEN MUSHROOM RAMEN

CHICKEN MUSHROOM CHOWDER & RAMEN NOODLES & COCONUT MILK
IT JUST GOT INTERESTING

NO, IT REALLY HAS!

HOW, WHERE, DID THESE 2 DISHES COLLIDE?

STEPS *HERE'S HOW TO ROCK THIS SHAKE-UP.*

1

- **IN A 3-QUART SAUCEPAN**, add the following to 2 C. of your warming Chowder
- Curry powder – about 2 Tbsp. for 4 – 6 servings

If you are making a smaller portion, use 1 Tbsp. – you can always add.

- 2 Tbsp. tomato paste
- 1 tablespoon of both grated ginger and grated or minced garlic.
- Canned coconut milk.

Give or take (again, depending the portions you're making), 7 oz. is usually a safe amount. Start on the lighter side. After tasting, add more if you enjoy a creamier/sweeter Curry.

- On the reverse, if you, your family & friends enjoy spice, let's talk Harissa:

Harissa is a Tunisian hot chili pepper garlic paste. You can find it in the international isle of your store, or of course online.

- I really enjoy spicy food, so I put in **2 Tbsp**., but if you prefer just a little heat, only add **1 Tbsp** – or don't use it at all. The curry powder has some spice to it.

Personally, I like the addition of Harissa. It balances the sweetness of the coconut milk.

2

- All this amazing Shake-Up needs to tie the dish together, is Ramen noodles.
- **DO NOT & I MEAN DO NOT**, cook the noodles in water prior to adding them to the pot of warmed Chowder.
- Natural Ramen comes packaged in proportionate servings.
- When I say Natural, I mean there is, nor ever will be, MSG in any of my recipes.

3

- Once your Chowder has reduced, turn the heat off. Add in 4 – 6 portions of Ramen (They will soak up all the tasty flavor from the Chowder & and all will become one.) **That's all she wrote!**

Grab a fork & or Chopsticks for the noodles & a big spoon for the Curry!

If it's been a rough day, this heartwarming dish will do just that, warm your heart!

SILKY CURRY RAMEN BOWL THE BOLD FLAVORS WILL IMPRESS!

CHICKEN MUSHROOM QUESADILLA

How many Quesadillas have you ordered in restaurants?
This one is made in
YOUR RESTAURANT (YOUR HOME)
GOOD INGREDIENTS, GOOD DISH, GOOD TIMES!

Sandwich?
NO WAY, when you can have these yummy Quesadillas!
This is not only better than sandwich night, but also even better than pizza night. **There, I said it!**

STEPS

1
- Start by toasting your flour tortillas in a medium-high skillet for **30 seconds** on each side & set them aside until it's time to assemble some Quesadillas.

2
- Warm 2 C. Chowder (4 – 6 portions) on low in a saucepan.

3
- Grate ½ C. Cheddar cheese, or the cheese of your choice & set aside until your Chowder is warm.

4
- Once the Chowder is warm, put in half of your grated cheese & stir for a couple minutes until it turns into melty goodness.
- That will take a good amount of time. By a good amount of time, I mean maybe **1 minute**!

5
- Layer the Chowder & cheesy mixture on top of the tortilla, add the rest of the grated cheese & top with the other tortilla.

6
- Into a 375 oven on a baking sheet for about **12 minutes**, it goes.
- You're just making sure everything is warm & the cheese is melted. When ready and out of the oven, chop the Quesadillas into quarters & garnish with Pico or salsa & crema (sour cream or Greek yogurt mixed with a squeeze of lime juice & a sprinkle of salt & pepper).

THESE ARE CRUNCHY ON THE OUTSIDE & UNBELIEVABLY SUCCULENT ON THE INSIDE. NOT TO MENTION THE BRIGHT SPICE OF THE PICO/SALSA ON TOP.

CHICKEN MUSHROOM BURRITO

STEPS

THIS IS HOW TO BURRITO!

1 Reduce 1 C. of your Chowder per for 4 – 6 Servings, (depending on the size of your tortillas), in a saucepan on low until it begins to cook down & thicken.

2 While the Chowder is reducing, slice 1 large onion into about ½ in. slices & sauté in a skillet with some olive oil until they just begin to soften.

3 **Tortillas** - warm them on the top of your stove, should you have gas. It only takes 3 seconds per side over the flame (using thongs).

If you have electric one, warm them in a dry skillet on the top of your stove, or you can stack them in between moistened paper towels & microwave for 15 seconds. The rest is as easy as it gets:

4 Top the reduced Chowder with grated cheese – Cheddar, Monterey Jack, Mexican blend, etc. & transfer it all to the tortillas using a big spoon.

CHOWDER REDUCING

5 Next the sautéed onions & then the final flavor punch – Pico de Gallo & crema.

If you don't want to make Pico, just use your favorite Pico or salsa from the store. If you want to make Pico & Crema, here you go... You can also see the full recipe on Page 50.

MESSY GOODNESS

PICO D' GALLO

- 3 Roma or vine-ripened tomatoes
- 1 small white onion or half of a medium one.
- 1 Jalapeno pepper or serrano if you like it on the hotter side.
- Juice of one lime.
- Salt & Pepper.
- Chopped or ripped cilantro if you like.
- Chop the onion into a small dice & let it rest in a bowl of cold water for **5 minutes**.

Cold water takes the sting out of onions – be sure to dry the onions before adding them to the Pico. Otherwise, you'll end up with a very watery Pico & we don't want that.

If you have a food Pro or even a blender, making Pico de Gallo takes minutes, as you can chop the veg into large pieces & the Pro or blender does the work for you.

CREMA

CREMA IS EVEN MORE CHALLENGING

- 1 C. Sour Cream or Greek Yogurt.
- Juice of 1 lime.
- Salt & Pepper to taste.
- Stir together – **DONE!**

****If the crema is too thick, thin it out a little by adding a small dash of water.***

NOT TO BE TOO CHEEKY, BUT THAT'S A WRAP!

CHICKEN MUSHROOM SKILLET

No need to even plate this dish, take it to the table & let everyone serve themselves.

HEARTWARMING FOOD!

For all intents & purposes, all you are doing is adding seared chicken to the Chowder. If you're not well versed in searing chicken, you will be shortly.

STEPS

AS PROMISED, HERE IS THE SUREFIRE WAY TO SEAR CHICKEN.

1 Before anything – make sure your chicken is out of the fridge for **30 minutes & at room temperatures**.

If your protein is NOT at room temperature & is cold, it will NOT cook through properly. The outside will sear or even burn & the inside will be raw.

SIMPLE TIP – BUT YOU'LL HAVE BETTER PROTEIN MOVING FORWARD SHOULD YOU GRASP ONTO & REMEMBER IT.

I prefer chicken thighs, but whether you are using thighs or breasts, this is an easy way to successfully achieve golden brown seared chicken.

***NOTE - Skin on chicken does not work here. No matter how well you sear the skin, it will get gummy once the Chowder is added to the chicken. The jus of the Chowder will negate all your effort to create that brown sear.**

2 This *SHAKE-UP* is done in one pot. To that heavy-bottomed pot, add a couple tablespoons of olive oil.

TIPS

- **Speaking chicken**, I personally prefer thighs. You almost have to try to overcook them.
- I completely get it if you want to use white meat instead. It takes less time to cook through, but it takes much more supervision so that it doesn't get too dry.

No matter what cut of chicken you choose, the jus of the CHOWDER will save you. If you need saving, that is.

3
- Turn the heat on medium. If the heat is too high, your chicken will burn. If it's on low, it will not achieve that beautiful golden brown.
- You'll know the oil is ready to sear the chicken when it thins out and moves easily by itself when you tilt the pot.

HERE'S THE END...

4
- Place your chicken in the pot & sear it for **3 minutes per side**.
- After the chicken is in the pot, don't & I mean **DON'T**, move it. Give it the **3 minutes** & then flip it to the other side for the remaining **3 minutes**.
- See, achieving golden brown chicken will never be difficult again!

THE REMAINDER OF THIS DISH IS INTENSE.

5
- To the seared chicken, pour in a couple cups of Chowder, warm on medium for **30 minutes & done**.

GET READY FOR THIS COMFORTING MEAL.

IT'S ABOUT TO HIT YOU - *IN A VERY GOOD WAY!*

TACO CHOWDER

You can hit ctrl alt delete, but this Chowder needs no rebooting!
Well, I guess if you don't love tacos with cheese & salsa.
Not to mention some crunchy chips to accompany.

INGREDIENTS

- 1 lb. Ground Beef or Turkey or a combination of both
- 1 tsp. Granulated Garlic
- ¼ tsp. Cayenne – Again, your call on the spice level.
- 2 Tbsp. Coriander
- 2 Tbsp. Cumin
- 2 Tbsp. Chili Powder

*** Sautee the spices with your ground meat. The spices will be beautifully bloomed (fragrant) by the time the meat is browned.**

JUICY POTATOES

- 3 Small or 2 medium Carrots
- 3 Celery Stocks
- 2 Garlic Cloves
- 2 - 3 Quarts Stock – some to keep the potatoes from sticking to the pot, the rest to finish the Chowder.
- 1x 28 oz. can of chopped or pureed Tomatoes – preferably San Marzano
- ½ C. Heavy Cream or Half & Half

FOR TOPPING THE BOWLS OF CHOWDER WHEN SERVING:

- Grated Monterey Jack, Cheddar, Fontina, Gouda, or any other nice melting cheese.
- Tortilla chips for dipping, shredded lettuce, a dollop of sour cream & homemade Pico de Gallo or jarred salsa.

All are delicious accompaniments.

TIPS

This Chowder doesn't need to be extra spicy (heat-wise), but it does need to include all the warming spices – Ground Cumin, Coriander, & Chili Powder. Otherwise, it will not resemble the tacos you know & love.

***Exclude Cayenne to negate spicy heat.**

TACOS IN A BOWL. MUCH EASIER TO EAT AND JUST AS, IF NOT MORE, FULFILLING

STEPS

1
- Begin by rendering down the bacon in your Dutch oven or another heavy bottomed pot.
- Remove the bacon from the pot with thongs onto paper towels, once it's rendered most of the fat.

2
- Chop the bacon into bite size pieces & set aside until you build the rest of the Chowder.

3
- Sauté your seasoned ground turkey or beef or chicken, or even firm tofu (if that's how you roll.) in the bacon renderings until it's just lightly browned & remove from the pot.

IT'S PARTY TIME – JUICY POTATOES!

4
- Put all the ingredients for **JUICY POTATOES (above & always Pg. 8)** in your pot & let them simmer down until the potatoes become tender-crisp. As I always say, don't let them go too far. We're not going for mashed potatoes.

Remember that they will continue to cook in the Chowder itself. It's also a time saver – don't we all need that?

Small chunks of potato are good in the finished Chowder, but personally, large chunks of potato in my Chowders are a **NO-GO. OTHER FLAVORS SHOULD SHINE - HAVE YOU EVER ORDERED, SAY, A CLAM CHOWDER & WHEN IT SHOWS UP, IT'S MAINLY CHUNKS OF POTATOES?**

YEA, NOT GOOD!

The potatoes are used as a thickener – don't get me wrong, the flavor doesn't hurt either.

Meat, JUICY POTAOTES, vegetables & spices together before incorporating liquids

5
- Now include the rest of the base to the **JUICY POTATOES** - bacon, browned meat, tomatoes & stock.
- Cook with the lid ajar for **45 minutes**.

Stock added & shortly some cream or half & half to polish off the Chowder.

6 If the Chowder isn't thick enough for you, take the lid off & simmer for another **15 minutes** or until it's to your liking.

7 Blush the Chowder with your half & half or heavy cream – off the heat so it doesn't curdle.

The final treat with this Chowder is whatever toppings you enjoy on your tacos – see suggestions in the ingredient list!

NOT SURE ABOUT YOU, BUT I DON'T WANT TO TALK ABOUT TACOS ANYMORE.

Just EAT!

What goes swimmingly with tacos?

MARGARITA

If you think Margaritas are difficult to make at home, let me assure you, it's very simple!

Four ingredients & it's fun Friday or any other day for that matter.

Here's how to make a beautiful Margarita:

- 2 parts Silver Tequila – of your choice.
- 1-part Cointreau
- Fresh lime juice from ½ - 1 lime
- Splash of good orange juice.
- Shake or stir it all together with a lot of ice.

IT'S TIME TO GET TOGETHER WITH

TACO CHOWDER & ICE-COLD MARGARITAS!

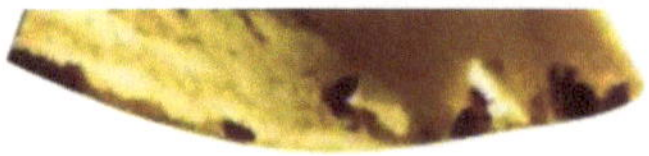

TACO CHOWDER *Shake Ups*

1. *Taco Omelet or Scramble*

2. *Taco Lettuce Wraps*

3. *Taco Stir-Fried Rice*

TACO OMELET OR SCRAMBLE

Your reduced Chowder about to have its moment.
A moment on your table that is.
That's about how long this dish will last!

Here's the Omelet Dance.
The Alternate – Scramble, Jives below as well.

STEPS

1

- Begin by vigorously scrambling your eggs in a large bowl with a whisk. Some believe in adding a Tbsp. or so of dairy (half & half or heavy cream) when whisking the eggs, but I don't think it's necessary.
- The eggs are whisked enough once you have copious amounts of bubbles on the surface of the bowl. It should only take a minute or so of whisking to achieve those bubbles.

2

- **Place the bowl** of whisked eggs aside and move on to what will be the filling of the omelet. That would be **CHOWDER…**

3

- **Warm the Chowder** in a saucepan on medium-low until it reduces a bit. You don't want a watery liquid inside an omelet. It won't take but **5 minutes** to thicken.

4

- Cheese - Now that your eggs are ready to cook and the Chowder is reducing, it's time to get the cheese ready. This is completely up to you.

I prefer cheddar, provolone, or gruyere in omelets, but you can use a simple American cheese if that's what you have. Sliced cheese makes for an easier process, but there's nothing wrong with grating a block of cheese, either.

LUXURY IN DISGUISE

LET'S TALK OMELETS

Most people are intimidated about making an omelet.

It does take some practice, but it's worth it.

I've been making simple omelets since I was a very young child & mine still come out with little imperfections – as you can see in the photos to your left.

Hey, homemade food is supposed to look just that - **HOMEMADE.**

The thing about making omelets, is that they don't need to be perfect. As long as you don't let the eggs go too far and brown on the bottom, it will be great.

If you don't want to take on omelets, no problem, just make a scramble instead.

Not to worry, I'll guide you.

5 Start the eggs, put 1 Tbsp. of butter and 1 Tbsp. of olive oil in an 8 ½ in. skillet – or around that size. You don't want an extra-large skillet – it makes it harder to fold out of the pan. Omelets aren't easy to make for a crowd, so I would suggest that you make this SHAKE-UP for 4 servings or less, as you can only make one at a time.

Once you finish an omelet, put it on a sheet pan, cover it in foil and place it into a 200-degree oven to keep warm while making the rest. It might sound like a big deal, but it really isn't. The eggs won't continue to cook, and the filling will stay nice and warm.

TIPS

*Plus, one 4 egg omelet can easily feed 2 people, so you may only need to make two – MAX three.
* With all that said, I know it can be intimidating to take on an omelet.

For a lot of Chefs, making a proper omelet is pass/fail as a candidate for Sous Chef – I've heard. You'll never hear me clam to be a Chef.
SO, if it's **NOT** something you want to achieve, throw together a tasty scramble instead

SCRAMBLE - Speaking of intimidating, check out these instructions...

1 Scramble eggs in a bowl.

2 Put them in a non-stick pan lined with 1 Tbsp. butter or Olive Oil.

3 Pour in your warm chowder & cheese.

4 Stir on medium low until the doneness of your liking.

WHETHER YOU OMELET OR SCRAMBLE THIS SHAKE-UP, THE RESULT REMAINS

SIMPLY IRRESISTIBLE!

TACO CHOWDER LETTUCE CUPS

It's not only a ridiculously delicious & fun dish but also gluten-free. If you're not gluten-free & are **NOT** into greens (**LIKE MY BROTHERS**), feel free to use corn or flour tortillas instead. I like them all, but what I like the most about using lettuce as a wrap is that you don't feel guilty about having 3 or more.

FOOD COMA – NOPE, NOT HAPPENING AFTER DEVOURING THIS DISH!

STEPS *Bring on another very tasty, speedy and cheap SHAKE-UP.*

1
- As usual, reduce 1 C. of your Chowder in a saucepan on low heat until it thickens and turns into more of a sauce.

Remember to stir the Chowder every few minutes – say about 3 – to be sure it isn't beginning to stick to the bottom of the pan. If at any point it starts to stick, turn the heat down.

2
- For these wraps, I prefer using Iceberg lettuce. It's sturdy and very crunchy, which holds up to the Chowder without making too much of a mess when eating them. Although, I see nothing wrong with Taco Chowder wraps running down my arms.

3
- Peel away 2 layers of the Iceberg for every wrap – doubling the leaves makes a big difference in flavor and structure.
- Take the reduced Chowder off the heat for about **5 minutes** so it isn't too hot for the lettuce – you want to uphold that beautiful crunch.
- When the Chowder is just warm, fill the lettuce wraps. Then move on to the toppings.

4
- Grated Cheese – Monterey Jack, Pepper Jack or Cheddar.
- Pico de Gallo or your favorite jarred salsa.
- Chopped Scallions – these aren't necessary because of all the onion flavor in the Chowder and the topping of Pico de Gallo or Salsa. It depends on how much of an onion lover you are.

Awesome dish anytime of the year, but especially fantastic in the summer.
Talk about a light & fun lunch or dinner

TIME TO GET YOUR CRUNCH ON - BE SURE TO HAVE YOUR NAPKINS READY!

SLOPPY FOOD IS GOOD!

TACO STIR-FRIED RICE

THIS SHAKE-UP MIGHT SOUND A LITTLE ODD, BUT THINK ABOUT IT...
When you get Tacos, Enchiladas, Burritos or most Mexican food, what do you typically get as a side?
RICE. What's wrong with combining the two?
I have the answer – nothing!

STEPS

LETS START THIS SHAKE-UP BY MAKING SOME SCRAMBLED EGGS.

1 Put a Tbsp. of olive oil/ butter or both in the bottom of a non-stick medium-sized skillet and turn the heat on to medium-low.

2 Whisk together 3 – 4 eggs in a bowl with a Tbsp. of Soy Sauce and a few dashes of hot sauce (or more if you enjoy spice.)

3 Put the whisked eggs into the skillet and stir with a spatula until they coagulate – it will only take about **3 - 4 minutes**.

4 Remove your pan from the heat and break up the cooked eggs into small pieces with your spatula - set aside.
Notes on RICE - Long grain rice is always best for fried rice – I prefer Jasmine. You can use any type of medium-sized saucepan (2 QT. is large enough) to make the rice, but I prefer non-stick due to the amount of starch in the rice. The non-stick pan will be a whole lot easier to clean.

5 For 4 – 6 servings put 1 ½ C. of rice & just a short (a couple Tbsp. short) of 3 C. of water or stock together in a saucepan.
***I think to result in a light fluffy rice, you should use a little less liquid than the package directions, hence the rice to liquid ratio suggested.**

6 Turn your heat on high until the stock and rice come to a boil. After it starts to boil, add a couple fat pinches of salt. Then turn it down to a low simmer and cover it with a lid to trap in the steam.

7 Simmer the rice for **2 – 3 minutes** less than the package directions. If you notice it simmering too vigorously, turn it down a bit. If the heat is too hot, the rice can easily burn on the bottom.

8 While the rice is simmering away, warm 1 C. of the Chowder in a small saucepan on low to cook down & reduce. Both the rice & Chowder should be done at about the same time.

Heading towards the finish line...

9

- Stir/sauté together the finished rice, reduced chowder & reserved scrambled eggs in a large skillet on high heat – or if you have a wok, you can use that as well. Only cook in the skillet for a minute or two – everything is already cooked. All your doing here is combining it all together.

Expanding your culinary horizons can sometimes result in a thing of delicious beauty - this SHAKE-UP being a perfect example!

Pull it all together if you'd like extra spice.

TOP YOUR DISHES WITH DICED SCALLIONS & OR SOME CILANTRO IF THAT'S THE WAY YOU LIKE TO DANCE!

BLACK BEAN JALAPENO CHOWDER

INGREDIENTS

- For the beans, fill a pot with water, add 1.lb. bag of black beans.
- Bring to a boil, turn off the heat, put on a lid & let sit for 1 hour.

If you prefer, you can use 4 cans of black beans instead of dried – just be sure to drain off the liquid.

REMAINING INGREDIENTS

- 1 lb. bacon

JUICY POTATOES

- 2 Russet potatoes
- 1 large or 2 medium onions
- 1 tsp. Thyme – fresh or dried
- 1 tsp. Rosemary – fresh
- 2 bay leaves
- ½ tsp. salt
- ¼ tsp. pepper

- 3 small or 2 medium carrots
- 3 celery stocks
- 2 Garlic cloves
- 1 tsp. Granulated garlic
- 1 tsp. Chili powder
- 1 tsp. Cumin
- 1 or 2 finely diced jalapenos
- 2 – 3 QT. Stock
- ½ C. Heavy Cream or Half & Half

STEPS

EASIEST CHOWDER RECIPE BY FAR!

1. Begin by sautéing 1 lb. bacon in a cast iron or heavy bottomed pot.
2. Once the bacon is rendered down, remove it from the pot onto paper towels & chop into bite size pieces.

As usual JUICY POTATOES come next...

3. In the bacon fat, cook the potatoes, onions & herbs, with splashes of stock every now and then to keep it not only from sticking, but to give the potatoes a place to give off some of their starch.
4. When the **JUICY POTATOES** are tender-crisp, add the chopped reserved bacon, vegetables, stock & beans.
5. Cook with the lid ajar on medium low for about **45 minutes** or until everything has come together.
   Be sure to check for seasoning. Both the potatoes & beans ask for a lot of salt & pepper.
   Once you're happy with the flavors and texture of everything, all that's left is to finish with your heavy cream or half & half.
   Top with the cheese of your choice and dip in.

TIPS

- For topping bowls of Chowder when serving:
- Grating of Cheddar, Monterey Jack or Pepper Jack Cheese are all great.

As you can see, I served this Chowder with a tomato grilled cheese instead of the cheese topper. To each their own, right!

IT MIGHT SOUND CRAZY SIMPLE. THERE'S A REASON FOR THAT – *IT IS!*

BLACK BEAN JALAPENO *Shake Ups*

1. Black Bean Enchiladas
2. Black Bean Tostadas
3. Black Bean Mac & Cheese

BLACK BEAN ENCHILADAS

Cheesy, tender Enchiladas right out of the oven.
It might take all your might to wait until these rest & set up, but in 10 minutes, you & your taste buds are going to be **VERY** happy!

MESSY YES. DELICIOUS YES!

STEPS — HERE'S THE ROUTE TO BLACK BEAN ENCHILADAS.

1

- **Preheat your oven to 375**.
- While your oven is heating, warm the Chowder in a small saucepan on medium low.
- You'll need approximately 2 C. for this *SHAKE-UP*. 1 ½ C. goes inside the Enchiladas and the other ½ C. goes on top to get all nice and bubbly.
- Make sure to strain the Chowder with a slotted spoon so that it isn't too soupy, otherwise your enchiladas will get soggy. Should the strained Chowder start to bubble vigorously and spit out of the pot or, even worse, on you, turn the heat down to low. We aren't doing anything than warming here.

PLUS – Black Bean Chowder can really burn you if it's popping out of the pot & it will also make a serious mess of your stove – no fun to clean.

2

- Line a baking sheet with foil and oil it so the enchiladas don't stick and make for easy removal from the pan.
- For 4 – 6 servings, a 9x9 in. baking sheet is perfect. Seven corn tortillas will snug up together nicely so that you don't have any empty space in the pan.
- It's best to put a bit of oil on both sides of the tortillas so they have less chance of cracking on you – they'll be more pliable.

Now for the ingredient that makes most happy – when it comes to enchiladas... Cheese

3

- Grate 2 C. Monterey Jack, Pepper Jack or a combination of both.
- You can always buy the already grated cheese in your grocery store. That way you get to skip the step. That's what this book is all about – **EASE**.

4

- Slather your strained black bean Chowder with the cheese into the corn tortillas, roll them, and place them as close together as possible into the pan.
- Don't do what I typically do and over stuff the tortillas. If you can't roll them easily, take some of the filling out. Otherwise, you'll end up with an enchilada casserole – not that there is anything wrong with that either.

THE HARDEST PART OF THIS SHAKE-UP:

5
- Buy enchilada sauce at your grocery store and pour it over the top of the rolled pan of enchiladas.
- You want the sauce to come to the top of the enchiladas. It seems like too much, but believe me, it's not.
- Red sauce or green tomatillo sauces are both quite good in stores today. Personally, I think a combination of both is delicious.

GREEN SAUCE/TOMATILLO SAUCE

RED/ROJA SAUCE

6
- Top with the rest of the grated cheese.

7
- Put foil over the pan and bake for **30 minutes**.

8
- After **30 minutes**, remove the foil and bake for another **15 minutes** or until the enchiladas are nice and bubbly around the edges.
- Just like any baked dish, **ALWAYS** let it rest for **10 minutes** once it comes out of the oven.
- Top with your favorite salsa and some sour cream if you'd like, once you've plated the dish – **YUM!**

Welcome to the easiest & cheapest homemade enchilada recipe. I'm hard pressed to not believe that this will become a staple in your cooking repertoire.

***NOTE: If you and your family are meat eaters, it takes no time to add browned ground meat or store-bought rotisserie chicken to the Black Bean Chowder - whether it be for the Chowder itself or just the enchiladas.**

MAKE IT YOUR OWN!

BLACK BEAN TOSTADAS

Crunchy, creamy, spicy, vibrant Tostadas, they hit all areas of your palate.

STEPS

1 Reduce 2 C. of the Chowder in a saucepan on low until it reduces enough that you can spread it onto the tostada. This should only take **5 – 10 minutes**.

2 While the Chowder is reducing, toast the corn tortillas in a 350-degree oven for about **5 minutes**. You can literally lay them on the rack of your oven, or you can put them on a baking sheet.

Check them after **5 minutes** & if they aren't crispy enough yet, give it a couple more minutes. Keep a close eye on them while they are in the oven. They go from crispy to burnt in no time.

3 Grate or slice the cheese of your choice. I like Pepper Jack or plain Monterey Jack for tostadas.

4 **As I've said so many times when making Mexican type dishes.**

Grab your homemade or store-bought Pico from the fridge & crema if you have some stored in there too. If not, combine sour cream or Greek yogurt with a squeeze of lime juice & a dash of salt & pepper. If it's too thick, thin it with a tiny bit (½ Tbsp.) of water or good chicken stock.

Time to build the Tostadas...

5 Slather some of the reduced Chowder onto the corn tortilla, top with cheese & put back into the warm oven for just a few seconds until the cheese melts.

Top the Chowder & cheese with Pico, crema, some lettuce if you want & a few leaves of cilantro.

NOTHING LEFT TO SAY...

IT'S TOSTADA TIME!

BLACK BEAN MAC & CHEESE

This SHAKE-UP can simply be a drop & stir dish if that's how your family enjoys Mac & Cheese. Or you can make it into a baked macaroni & cheese if that's your preference

STEPS

By drop & stir, see what I mean here...

1

- **QUICK & DIRTY** - Take some of the Black Bean Chowder and warm it with a couple blocks of processed cheese. We all know what I'm referencing to here. It's not how I roll, but in this instance, processed cheese just works. You want about 2/3 C. of cheese to 1/3 C. of Chowder. I recommend adding 1 C. grated cheddar for extra flavor.
- Boil 1 lb. short pasta your choice – macaroni, penne, cavatappi – in salted water **2 minutes** less than the package directions. If you want to make a stove top Mac & Cheese, you're **DONE!**

MIX TOGETHER, BOWL UP AND INDULGE.

Enter the baked version:

2

- **MIX TOGETHER** the black bean Chowder, cheese & pasta - Pour into a buttered casserole dish. Top with a mixture of Panko breadcrumbs, grated Parmesan cheese & 2 TBSP. of melted butter. Here's the topping...
- Melt 2 Tbsp. butter in a pan on low. Take off the heat & add ½ C. panko & ¼ C. grated parmesan.
- Place your topped Mac & Cheese in a **375** oven in whatever vessel you wish. You can use a casserole dish for 4 to 6 portions or, if you are only making it for 2 people, you can use an oven safe bowl & share.
- There's caring in sharing, right? The other option is to use ramekins & make individual dishes.
- It shouldn't take much time at all if the pasta and cheese sauce are already warm – approximately **15 – 20 minutes**, or until you see those gorgeous bubbles around the edge.
- The baked version of this recipe could be made ahead of time and stored in the refrigerator for days until you are ready to warm it in the oven. It will take closer to **45 minutes** to heat up if you are taking it straight from the refrigerator to the oven.

Either way you choose to prepare this Mac & Cheese, it turns out darn good!

YOU CAN'T REFUTE THE EASE OF BOTH BLACK BEAN CHOWDER *SHAKE-UPS!*

PULLED PORK CHOWDER

Store bought tortilla chips topped with reduced pulled pork Chowder, cheese of your choice & some scallions for freshness. **Fast Dinner!**

-OR-

HEY, LET'S GET TOGETHER for **A** reason or **NO** reason at all.

WHY NOT?

INGREDIENTS & STEPS

With Pulled Pork Chowder, Pork Shoulder/butt is the best choice.

For this recipe – 4 lbs.is a proper amount.

1

Take the pork out of the fridge & season with the following:

- 3 Tbsp. coarse salt
- 2 Tbsp. black pepper
- 2 Tbsp. dry mustard
- 1 Tbsp. garlic powder
- 1 Tbsp. onion powder
- 3 Tbsp. paprika – sweet or smoked

- I think it's best to used smoked. t's a much deeper flavor & with the amount of pork, all the veggies & the addition of half & half or heavy cream at the end, mellows out the spice.
- Rub the seasoning all over the entire surface of the pork.
- Allow the meat to sit in your fridge for at least **1 hour**, or overnight – that's best. It gives the brine time to infuse into/become one with the meat.

Remember to take the pork out of the fridge and let it come to room temp – about an hour before putting it in the oven to roast.

The only negative (if there is one), to this Chowder is time. It's takes 4 – 6 hours. With that said, the waiting time on brining & cooking the pork, is exactly that, WAITING.

You don't have to do anything while it's in the oven.

2

- Once the pork has brined & come to room temperature, place it in your Dutch oven & include the following to create a flavorsome barbeque sauce:

- ½ C. ketchup
- 1 C. yellow mustard
- 1 C. apple cider vinegar
- 2 – 3 garlic cloves – grated or smashed
- 1 Tbsp. salt
- ½ Tbsp. pepper
- ½ C. packed brown sugar - light or dark
- 2 C. chicken stock

3

- Roast the pork in your large enamel cast iron pot/Dutch oven or roasting pan (lid or foil on) at **325** for, as I said **4 – 6 hours**.
- Check after **4 hours** with a fork & if it falls apart easily, it's done.
- If there is still some resistance, let it bake for **another hour or 2**.

RECIPE ALTERNATIVE NEXT...

YOU CAN ALSO MAKE THE PORK SHOULDER IN A SLOW COOKER IF YOU HAVE ONE.

Set it on medium low & let it ride for **4 hours**.
The reason I like making it in a Dutch oven, is because the entire Chowder will be made in that one pot. Why have to clean your slow cooker as well?
Plus – I don't own a slow cooker. It takes up too much room in my small kitchen.
That's all she wrote for now.

4

- After the pork comes out of the oven & is resting aside on a large plate or cutting board, make the **JUICY POTATOES** in the same pot.

This is the only Chowder where I see no need for bacon. I think we're heavy enough on the pork the way it is. With that said, feel free to render 12 – 16 oz. of Bacon prior to making your...

JUICY POTATOES

- 2 large Russet Potatoes - sliced
- 1 Large or 2 medium Onions - diced
- 1 tsp. Thyme – fresh or dried - minced
- 1 tsp. Rosemary – fresh - minced
- 2 Garlic Cloves – minced or grated
- 2 Bay leaves
- 1 tsp. Salt
- ½ tsp. Pepper

5

- Once the **JUICY POTATOES** are done – **10 minutes**, incorporate your celery & carrots.
- 2 stalks celery – chopped.
- 2 large or 3 small carrots – chopped.

6

- Pull the pork apart with 2 forks, in as thin or thick pieces you like. Because this is for a Chowder, I prefer the pork shredded in thin strands so that everything in the Chowder will fit on your spoon, as you can see in the accompanied photo.

7

- Add 2 QT. Chicken Stock, put the lid back on the pot (ajar) & let it all come together for another **1 -2 hours**.
- After an hour, stir the Chowder to see if the **JUICY POTATOES** have broken down & thickened the pot of goodness.
- And as always, taste for seasoning. If it's not thick enough to your liking...
- Give it another **30 minutes** to an hour without the lid, what's the hurt?

You can do the dishes, laundry, or take a warm bath or shower while the chowder finishes.

- Right before serving, off the heat, pour in your half & half or heavy cream – ½ - 1 C. – depends how creamy you like your chowder.

THIS IS ONE STICK-TO-YOUR-RIBS LUXURIOUS CHOWDER!

PULLED PORK *Shake Ups*

1. *Pulled Pork Fried Rice*
2. *Pulled Pork Sandwich*
3. *Buffalo Pulled Pork Sandwich or Lettuce Wraps*

Making Pulled Pork Chowder may have taken some time.

Time well spent once your workweek is up & running.

Don't miss out on the opportunity.

Let these piggy Shake-Ups run run run all the way home...

To your home table, that is!

PULLED PORK FRIED RICE

15 – 20 MINUTES ANYTIME MEAL. SALTY, SWEET HEAVENLY GOODNESS	*THE FLAVOR POSSIBILITIES ARE ENDLESS.*	*IF YOU'RE A FRIED-RICE FAN & REGULARLY ORDER TAKE AWAY, THIS WILL CHANGE YOUR HABITS FOREVER!*

STEPS

HERE'S YOUR HOMEMADE TAKEAWAY...

1
- Warm 1 C. of the Pulled pork Chowder in a medium sized saucepan on low.
- It will only take about **10 minutes** for the Chowder to reduce.

2
- While that's happening, make your long grain rice to package directions, just **2 minutes** short so it remains al dente.

3
- Once your rice is done, sprinkle in some frozen peas – as much as you like.

I added some chopped fresh broccoli to this dish because I had it, but feel free to use whatever vegetable you enjoy in a good stir-fry.

Reduced Chowder with the addition of some chopped raw broccoli.

DON'T JUDGE ME!

4
- Stir the warmed Chowder & rice together & dinner's ready.

*Hint – dash some soy or tamari on top as well – gives the dish a lift!

It's not a bad idea to eat this dish in front of the TV, should there be something on you don't want to miss.

Who doesn't enjoy a Great Game, Show or Movie with some fried rice?

It might be contentious to some, but I'll eat this bowl of deliciousness with a spoon instead of chopsticks or even a fork.

NOT ONLY BETTER,

BUT HEALTHIER THAN TAKEAWAY!

PULLED PORK SANDWICH

Warmed pulled pork
Chowder & coleslaw
on a supple roll.

THIS IS NOT ONLY FOR WARMER MONTHS.

It's a delight in the cool/colder months too

THIS SANDWICH IS GOING TO RUN DOWN YOUR CHINNY CHIN CHIN

MAKE SURE YOU HAVE PLENTY OF NAPKINS

CRUNCHY COLESLAW

FRESH HOMEMADE COLESLAW

Before you start the coleslaw, warm & render down your Pork Chowder (2 C. for 4 portions). It takes no time as you want a good amount of jus for the drippy sandwich.

As for the Coleslaw. I'm not a sugar person, so my coleslaw is on the tangy side. Give the recipe a go. I think you'll be pleased.

INGREDIENTS

- ½ C. Mayo
- ½ C. Greek yogurt or sour cream
- 3 Tbsp. Dijon mustard
- 2 Tbsp. Red wine or Apple cider vinegar
- 2 Tbsp. white sugar
- 1 tsp. salt
- 1 tsp. pepper

STEPS

DRESSING

****NOTE – you can also use honey or agave as a sweetener – just keep in mind that agave is sweeter than sugar, so you might want to scale it back at first.***

1

- You can always add some more after tasting the dressing.
- Few dashes of hot sauce (optional), but I think it brightens the slaw.
- Whisk everything together & taste for seasoning/flavor.
- Season with more salt, pepper or sweetener if you'd like.

TIPS

***NOTE –** You want the dressing to have a deep flavor due to all the water in the cabbage. Once the salt & acid in the dressing hits the cabbage, it will release a good amount of moisture & bring the salad together.

COLESLAW

- Half head green cabbage
- Half Head Red Cabbage
- ½ C. Shredded Carrots
- 3 – 4 Scallions (diced) – depending on your liking of raw onions.

****Or you can do what a lot of people do these days & just purchase the pre-chopped & bagged Coleslaw mix from the grocery.***
Nobody will know – especially if you make your own dressing.

2

- Using a Sharp Knife, Box Grater OR the shredding attachment of your food processor if you have one, shred the carrots & cabbage.

3

- In a large bowl, mix everything together & let it sit on your counter for an hour or even more.
- Mix it around every now & then so all the dressing doesn't just settle on the bottom.

****NOTE – If you are taking this to an outside party in the summer, it must be kept on ice due to the Mayo. Otherwise, it can sit inside on your counter for the duration of your dinner/party.***

PILE YOUR WARMED PORK CHOWDER ONTO THE SOFT ROLLS & TOP WITH THE DELICIOUS COLESLAW.

FRESHLY MADE COLESLAW

Creamy, tangy, crunchy & spicy!

MAKE MORE OF THIS THAN YOU NEED FOR THE SAMMY'S

IT'S A WONDERFUL SIDE FOR MOST ANY PROTEIN.

SUCCLENT PORK & CRUNCHY SLAW ON A SOFT ROLL –

THESE SAMMIES WILL MAKE YOUR DAY!

BUFFALO SANDWICH OR LETTUCE WRAPS

This *SHAKE-UP* is an excellent quick & easy weeknight meal & perfect for friends and/or family get togethers. It takes **LESS THAN 15 MINUTES** to prepare & both the sandwich & lettuce wraps are great hot and at room temperature.

Put the food out, your feet up & ENJOY!

STACK *CHOWDER/HOT SAUCE MIXTURE ONTO YOUR ROLLS & OR LETTUCE.*
TOP *WITH BLUE CHEESE CRUMBLES, CHOPPED CARROTS & CELERY.*
GO FOR IT!

STEPS

1

- As is usual, warm your Chowder **(1 C.)** in a saucepan on medium low – just until it's warmed through.
- **ROLLS** for this dish - soft Kaiser rolls are perfect, but use any supple roll you want.
- **CHEESE** - Use your favorite blue cheese. You can crumble it yourself from block form or get it already crumbled.

Personally, I like a milder blue cheese for this preparation - Gorgonzola or Danish Blue. As you can see in the photo, I topped the sandwiches & wraps with chopped carrots. You can also chop up some celery & toss that on as well. I just didn't have any in the fridge.

Think of what you always get on the side of your wings – makes sense right?

2

- Using a slotted spoon, remove the Chowder to a bowl & add your hot sauce. The amount of hot sauce is touchy. Some like it mild & some like it **HOT**.
- I like it **HOT**, so I add a good ¼ C. If you like it mild, only add a couple Tbsp.

Also, use whatever hot sauce you favor. For the most part, they are all good quality today.

WHO DOESN'T LOVE ANYTHING BUFFALO?
ESPECIALLY WHEN IT'S SHOWERED WITH CRUMBLED BLUE CHEESE!

GET MESSY! **THERE'S NO SHAME IN THAT!**

CORN PORK CHOWDER

INGREDIENTS

STEPS

BASE/DNA

- 1 lb. Bacon
- 1 lb. Ground Pork

1 Render 1 lb. Bacon, remove from the pot & set aside. Chop into bite size pieces.

NEXT IS THE INEVITABLE WITH ALL CHOWDERS

2 Sear the ground pork in the rendered bacon fat until it's golden – remember to season every layer with S&P.
Do the same as with the bacon & remove the pork from the pot when seared. The pork will fully cook through in the Chowder.

JUICY POTATOES

- 2 large Russet Potatoes - sliced
- 1 Large or 2 medium Onions - diced
- 1 tsp. Thyme – fresh or dried, minced
- 1 tsp. Rosemary – fresh – finely diced
- 2 Bay leaves
- 1 tsp. Salt
- ½ tsp. Pepper

3 Sauté everything together on medium heat with some olive oil & splashes of stock to keep the potatoes from sticking. They'll be done in only **10 minutes**.

Details on Pg. 8.

JUICY POTATO directions are everywhere.

WHY NOT?

EVERYONE SHOULD KNOW HOW TO MAKE THEM!

REMAINING INGREDIENTS

- 3 Small or 2 medium Carrots – chopped small
- 3 Celery Stocks – chopped small
- 6 Fresh Corn cobbs – if it's in season. If not, add 1 ½ lb. of frozen corn.
- 2 Quarts Chicken Stock
- 1 C. Heavy Cream or Half and Half

4 After you are done with the **JUICY POTATOES**, all that's left is to add the remainder of the **DNA:**

HANG ON FOR A FEW MORE DETAILS TO HELP FINISH THIS

SWEET BEAUTY...

SWEET, BRIGHT, CRUNCHY CORN WITH RICH SCRUMPTIOUS GROUND PORK

WHAT? HUH? I'M NOT HATING IT!

5 Adding fresh basil on top when you are ready to serve makes for not only **BRIGHT FRESH FLAVOR**, but a **WOW** presentation!

TALK ABOUT A MATCH MADE IN HEAVEN!

AS PROMISED

FINISHED BOWLED CORN PORK CHOWDER

as mentioned on the first pages **(Pg. 11)**

HERE'S THE JPS

While there is some bacon fat in the pot,
I think it's best to add
1 Tbsp. olive oil as well to begin the
JUICY POTOTOES!
Due to all the starch in potatoes, they will easily stick to the bottom of your pot.
You can/SHOULD also add a couple Tbsp. of butter for flavor if you'd like.
Let's be honest, butter makes everything better, doesn't it?
Adding splashes of chicken stock while the potatoes & onions cook down will prevent them from sticking as well.
To your pot, on medium low heat, add the potatoes, onions, herbs, salt & pepper.
As I say, when the potatoes & onions are tender-crisp & somewhat silky (but not turning into mashed potatoes,) you're there.
THE JUICY POTATOES WILL FINISH DOING THEIR JOB AS THE CHOWDER COOKS.
THEIR FLAVOR & SILKYNESS ALWAYS BRINGS IT ALL HOME!

CORN PORK *Shake Ups*

1. *Corn & Pork Quiche*
2. *Corn Ratatouille*
3. *Corn & Pork Frittata*

CORN & PORK QUICHE

A LOVELY LIGHT DISH FOR ANYTIME OF THE DAY.

Great with a side salad as pictured below. Roasted vegetables, potato salad or macaroni salad are nice with this dish as well.
Really, any side you like will be delightful with this **QUICHE**.

STEPS

This corn, pork Shake-Up starts with a great ***SURPRISE.***
There is no need to render down the Chowder!

1
- What IS needed is to warm the Chowder (about 1 C.), in a saucepan for **5 minutes** on low.
- Having some liquid from the Chowder, combined with the eggs is a good thing.
- It almost turns into a custard. But it's even tastier due to the Chowder.
- **Preheat your oven to 400**.

For an ultra-quick breakfast, lunch, dinner, or brunch for that matter, simply buy store-bought frozen pie crust. Just follow the package directions.

2
- Whatever you do, **DON'T** skip the step of docking the pie dough with a fork on the bottom and sides of the crust prior to baking. The steam needs to release while par baking.

3
- Whisk together 5 eggs (for 4 – 6 servings), in a large bowl with a couple pinches of salt and pepper.
- If you love a **LITTLE KICK OF SPICE**, add a few dashes **(6 OR SO)** of your favorite hot sauce. **OR** if you enjoy spice like I do, add ¼ C. & get a **DIRECT KICK TO THE FACE**.

4
- You can't have a Quiche without cheese. Even if your Vegan, please SUB with your favorite "cheese".

In this dish I really prefer Swiss, but you can use whatever cheese you enjoy – Swiss, Cheddar, Muenster, etc.

You can't go wrong!
TIME SAVER - You can always use already grated store bought packaged cheese.

Here's where it all comes together.

5 Into the bowl of whisked eggs, mix together your warmed Chowder and cheese.

6 Line a sheet pan with foil.

7
- Pour the egg mixture into your par cooked pie crust and put it back into the oven for another **35 minutes** or until the eggs are set up.
- Check the quiche after **30 minutes** – it might be done.
- When it's done, it will be puffed up like a soufflé. Once you take it out of the oven, it will deflate a bit, but that's normal.

THESE FLAVORS COME TOGETHER SWIMMINGLY.

The beauty of this dish is the ease of preparation, and that it can be eaten hot, warm, room temperature or even cold (for leftovers), right out of the refrigerator.

CORN PORK CHOWDER

WHISKED EGGS

CHEESE

PAR-COOKED PIE CRUST

AN EASY & ECONOMICAL WAY TO TRANSPORT YOURSELF TO A PARISIAN BISTRO!

CORN & PORK RATATOUILLE

Ratatouille isn't one of those dishes that's on a regular household menu for most.
but with assistance from your Chowder, this dish is much simpler than it looks.
And wow – the flavor is packed!
If you haven't had the pleasure of enjoying Ratatouille, you're in for a gratifying experience!

STEPS

1

- Warm your Chowder in a saucepan on low – 1 ½ C. will be enough.

2

- Sear 1 or 2 Italian sausage links in a skillet (sweet or hot). it all depends on how may portions you are making.1 link is plenty for 4 portions & 2 is great for 6 – Remember, you already have pork in the Chowder.
- With the hopes of not making a mess of your stove, keep the heat on medium low with a lid ajar or a piece of foil on top & Add splashes of water if the pan begins to dry out – sausage needs moisture to cook through properly.

3

- Chop the sausage into small pieces once it's done & let sit aside until everything else is ready.

4

- Time to dice a couple tomatoes – be sure to seed them. The seeds tend to be bitter.
- **As for the edamame**, if you're using frozen in pods, all you need to do is soak them for **5 minutes** in hot water.
- Squeezing them out of the pods is nothing, really but it does take **a couple minutes**.
- Even easier, purchase them frozen - already out of their pods.

5

- All that's left to do is open the package & pour into the skillet.
- **CORN** - depends on the time of the year and where you live (of course).
- The best choice is fresh corn, but you can always use frozen.

THIS IS CONTROVERSIAL FOR MANY PEOPLE, but when fresh corn is available, **I NEVER boil it**.
I either sear it right on the top of the gas stove for **10 seconds** on each side, sear it on a grill, or keep it completely raw. If you boil it, the crunchy sweetness & nutrients of your corn will be all left in the boiling water (that you toss) instead of on your plate.
Ok, I'll get off my soapbox - that's that...

Put everything in the pan with the Chowder, mix together & **YOU'RE DONE!**
For as simple as this dish is, the flavors say something else.

WHAT IS IT THAT, YOU ASK?

IT'S SIMPLE. USE QUALITY INGREDIENTS (BEST YOU CAN FIND),

THE RESULT IS JUST THAT - QUALITY DISHES!

CORN & PORK FRITTATA

PERFECT DISH FOR ANYTIME OF THE DAY!

STEPS *HERE'S THE SIMPLE PREPARATION*

FRITTATAS – SILKY EGGY GOODNESS!

1 **Warm your oven to 375**.

2 Whisk 6 eggs together in a bowl for 4 servings. Add 2 more eggs for 6 servings.

3 Warm the Chowder (1 C.), in a nonstick sauté pan. This way you have less cleanup, since you're making the Frittata in a sauté pan anyway.

4 Grate ½ C. Cheese (cheddar is great here), into the whisked eggs & join the Chowder & eggs together in the pan.

5 On low heat, stir the egg Chowder mixture lightly with a rubber spatula until the eggs start to set up a bit on the edges of the pan. This will only take **3 minutes**.

What's left?

6 Put the pan in the oven topped with a grating of Parmigiana & let the Frittata finish cooking through **10 minutes** should do it.
When the eggs no longer jiggle in the pan, it's perfectly done.

There truly is no need for a side with this dish, but if you would like one, a simple arugula salad dressed with fresh lemon juice, olive oil & salt is a good call.

A nice grating of Parmesan cheese will take it over the top!

EAT THIS HOT, WARM, ROOM TEMPERATURE, OR COLD.

BELIEVE ME, IT WORKS!

CHICKEN AMERICAN DIP CHOWDER

INGREDIENTS

BASE/DNA

- 1 lb. Bacon – chopped
- 1 3-4 lb. Rotisserie Chicken

JUICY POTATOES

- 2 large Russet Potatoes
- 1 Large or 2 medium Onions
- 1 tsp. Thyme – fresh or dried
- 1 tsp. Rosemary – fresh
- 2 Bay leaves
- 1 tsp. Salt
- ½ tsp. Pepper
- 3 Tbsp. Chicken Base

REMAINING INGREDIENTS

- 3 Small or 2 medium Carrots
- 3 Celery Stocks
- 2 Garlic Cloves
- 2 Quarts Chicken Stock
- Few dashes of Worcestershire
- Couple dashes of Soy or Tamari
- 1 C. Heavy Cream or Half and Half

STEPS

1

- As with most Chowders, begin by sautéing the bacon in your cast iron or heavy bottomed pot.
- When the bacon has rendered out most of it's fat, remove it with thongs - place on paper towels & chop into bite size pieces.

2

- While the bacon is rendering, pull your chicken off the bones, but keep it in bite sized pieces. You don't want it shredded – you'll lose it in the Chowder if the pieces aren't intact.

NOTE - For me, the skin on the chicken is a no go. It just gets gummy in the Chowder, but hey, that's your call.

3

Note regarding chicken base - To the chicken, sprinkle on 3 Tbsp. Chicken Base (sometimes called Broth Base), salt & pepper. It comes in powdered form.

- If you can't find it in your store, you can get it online. If all else fails, get the best quality Chicken Bouillon available.
- Sauté the chicken on low for **2 minutes**, in your pot with a small amount of bacon fat - 2 Tbsp. – discard the rest.
- Incorporate 1 Qt. Chicken stock, the Worcestershire & soy/tamari. This is the jus.
- Check for seasoning - salt, pepper, spice, umami, texture – add whatever will round out the flavor. It should be bright & strong.

The JUICY POTATOES will pull it all together

4

- I know there is some bacon fat in the pot but add 1 Tbsp. olive oil as well. Due to all the starch in potatoes, they will easily stick to the bottom of your pot.
- Adding splashes of chicken stock while the potatoes & onions cook down will prevent the sticking & burning as well. To your pot, on medium low heat, add the potatoes, onions, herbs, garlic, salt & pepper.

See exact amounts on Pg. 8 & EVERYWHERE ELSE – Can't refute it!

- If you'd like, add a couple Tbsp. of butter for flavor. This is optional.
- Cook the **JUICY POTATOES** down until the potatoes begin to give off their starch & become tender-crisp & somewhat creamy. This takes about **10 minutes**.

- To the creamy, silky **JUICY POTATOES**, it's time to marry everything in the pot:
- Bacon, carrots, celery – season with salt & pepper & add the stock.

Note – Seasoning with salt & pepper every time you add an ingredient, will result in a much tastier & well-rounded flavor.

5

- Put a lid onto the pot – ajar and cook on medium low for approximately **45 minutes** to an hour. Check to be sure that it's not bubbling too much, you're looking for a light simmer.
- Taste for seasoning & texture. If it's still on the thin side take the lid off and cook for another **5 – 10 minutes**.
- Off the heat, finish with room temperature heavy cream or half & half.
- Taste it again, for seasoning & add a dash of cayenne if you would like – I certainly do.

WHO NEEDS AN MSG DIPPER WHEN YOU CAN ENJOY THIS FLAVORFUL ALL-NATURAL JUS?

HOPEFULLY, YOU'LL BE INSPIRED TO RID OF ARTIFICIAL INGREIDENTS.

YOUR BODY WILL BE HAPPIER & THANK YOU – *PROMISE!*

CHICKEN AMERICAN *Shake Ups*

1. Chicken American Dip Sandwich

2. Fettuccini with Chicken, Bacon & Peas

3. Chicken Broccoli Cheese Bake

CHICKEN AMERICAN DIP SANDWICH

If you like a French dip, this *SHAKE-UP* will blow your mind... I'm not kidding!
My husband thinks this is WAY better than the typical Beef French Dip & I happen to whole heartedly agree.

STEPS - *TO SLOPPY, DRIPPY AMERICAN DIP SANDWICHES*

From the store, grab nice soft sub rolls.
This is a dish where a hard-tough roll will not work – believe me!
***FRIES** - See the note at the bottom of the recipe.

1

- **FOR THE JUS** - Warm 1 C. of your Chowder in a small saucepan on low heat.

To the Chowder, add the following:

- 1 TBSP. Worcestershire and 1 TBSP. Tamari or Soy sauce
- ½ to ¾ C. Low Sodium Chicken Stock – add more if needed to thin the Chowder until it becomes a jus (think of the texture of broth.)
- Cook it down uncovered until you like the texture & of course, taste for proper seasoning – won't be more than **5 minutes**.

2

- While the jus is coming together, it's a good time to make the boneless skinless chicken breast.
- Put about 1 TBSP. of olive oil in a non-stick skillet and warm on medium heat – see note below about how to ensure you end up with tender and moist chicken breast.

****Note – always, and I mean always, take your chicken out of the refrigerator at least 30 minutes before you are going to cook it. If you put cold protein in a hot skillet, the outside will brown & sear & the inside will still be raw – not ideal.***

Also, season the chicken (after you pat it dry with paper towels), with salt & pepper when you remove it from the fridge. The seasoning creates a dry brine so that when you hear it in the pan, it creates a nice brown crust.

GOLDEN BROWN CHICKEN BREAST IS GOOD!

3

- After **10 or so minutes** have passed, heat your skillet to medium. Now, place the chicken breasts into the oiled skillet (1 – 2 TBSP. of olive oil).
- It takes about **4 minutes** per side to cook a good-sized chicken breast. It seems today that they are quite large.
- After you take the chicken out of the pan, let it rest for a good **5 – 10 minutes** before slicing it. That way you don't lose the juices & the chicken ends up nice and moist. Ok, everything should be ready to come together...

- Pour the jus into a bowl for dipping.
- Slice the chicken – not too thin & not too thick. Using thongs, run the sliced chicken through the jus for flavor & moisture.
- Fill the rolls with the drippy chicken & your Chicken American Dip Sandwich is ready.

You'll polish this off in no time – **PROMISE!** My husband is a good, but typically a slow eater & he inhaled it!

4

***Note on the fries: For ease & convenience, grab a bag of hand cut fries from the freezer section of your grocery store.**

- Bake them on a foil lined baking sheet according to the package directions.
- Once the fries are done, immediately put them into a large bowl and sprinkle them with Old Bay seasoning and toss so the fries are seasoned well.
- If for whatever reason, you aren't an Old Bay fan, use whatever you prefer. Powdered Ranch seasoning can work here, or you can just salt & pepper the fries & leave it at that.

It's all good!

If you let the fries cool a little, the seasoning – no matter what you choose to use, will not stick to the fries.
You'll be left with bare fries and the seasoning sitting on the bottom of the bowl.

WE ALL CAN USE A LITTLE
EXTRA SPICE IN LIFE!

CHICKEN AMERICAN FETTUCCINI

SHAKE IT UP WITH FETTUCCINE CHICKEN, BACON & PEAS

STEPS

1

- For 4 – 6 servings, warm 1. C of your Chowder in a saucepan on medium low until it reduces by ½. **This should take 10 – 15 minutes.**

2

- Bring a large pot of water (6 QT.), to a boil so that it's waiting on you & you're not waiting on it.

When it comes to bacon, I typically have cooked bacon in the fridge that I just chop into bite size pieces.

3

- If you don't, sear (½ lb.) on medium low in a sauté pan until it's the doneness of your liking & chop into pieces.
- My taste in bacon is a bit different than many others. I like my bacon to have a little meaty chew. Extra crispy burnt bacon bits don't work for me.
- The bacon & Chowder should be ready about the same time.

IN THE PAN ON THE STOVE

4

- Heavily salt your pot of pasta water – at least 2 Tbsp., if not more.

****Reminder – Don't salt your water prior to it coming to a boil. Otherwise, it will scorch the bottom of your pot.***

- Boil 1 lb. fettucine **2 minutes** short of package instructions.
- The pasta will carry over cook when you put the Chowder, bacon & peas all together.

PLATED with GRATED PARM

5
- Right before you drain the pasta, spoon out some starchy water into a bowl or mug in case you need to loosen the sauce.
- Due to the Chowder, you might not need any, but it's best to have just in case. The water is all going down the drain anyway,

6
- While the pasta is cooking, grate about ½ C. Parmesan cheese.
- Stir most of it into the Fettucine dish & use the rest to top with a sprinkling when plating.

7
- Combine the drained pasta, reduced Chowder, chopped bacon, ½ C. frozen peas – (No need to defrost) & your grated Parm cheese in the large pasta pot.
- Stir it all together & what you have is a very flavorful meal for anytime of the week.

I love pasta!

IF YOU DO, THIS DISH WILL MOST CERTAINLY NOT DISAPPOINT!

CHICKEN BROCCOLI CHEESE BAKE

CHOWDER	DECADENCE WE ALL SHOULD SALUTE!	BROCCOLI
CHICKEN		CHEESE

STEPS

1
- For 4 – 6 servings, warm 1. C of your Chowder in a saucepan on medium low until it reduces by about ½. It will take around **10 minutes**.
- **Preheat your oven to 375**.

2
- While that's happening, chop 1 large or 2 small broccoli heads into bite size florets

3
- Bring a medium size pot (3 Qt.) of water to a boil for the pasta.
- Once it comes to a boil, heavily salt the water & add pasta of choice. I used Cavatappi – because I love it, which is why I had it in the pantry.
- Use whatever short pasta you want.
- For this dish, it is VERY important that you only cook the pasta for **2 – 3 minutes**.

4
- **MIX TOGETHER**: Reduced Chowder, **JUICY POTATOES**, Veggies
- Cheese – ½ C. Parmesan
- ½ C. grated Sharp Provolone
- The pasta & raw broccoli will cook through properly after baking in the oven & resting on the counter for **10 minutes**.
- Keep ¼ C. Cheese for topping the bake.

As you can see, I also pulled some sliced Provolone & placed it on top before baking – not necessary, but nice touch.

SMOOTH AMERICAN DIP CHOWDER
TWO VARIETIES OF CHEESE PASTA
BEAUTIFUL BROCCOLI FLORETS

THIS IS A SERIOUS BELLY PLEASER!

- Be sure to lightly coat your baking dish with some oil – olive or whatever you have so it's easy to remove & plate.
- Bake for **30 – 40 minutes**.

5

When there are bubbles around the edges of your pan, it's time to take it out of the oven & let it rest.

As I mentioned for 10 minutes.

- This bake just might change your mind about (casserole night).
- Nothing from a can – all fresh.
- Think broccoli cheese soup in bake form – but WAY better.

**IF THERE ARE ANY LEFTOVERS,
BE FIRST TO THE
FRIDGE TOMORROW!**

ANOTHER WAY TO GET YOUR KIDS OR ADULTS IN YOUR LIFE TO EAT THEIR VEGGIES.

BRING ON THE BROCCOLI!

CHICKEN PORK MEATBALL CHOWDER

Not that all Chowders aren't, but this Meatball Chowder is perfect for the couch – especially if it's fall or winter. It's soupy, it's meaty & it's hearty. Can't go wrong with that combination!

INGREDIENTS & STEPS

HERE'S HOW YOU ROLL OUT THIS MEATBALL CHOWDER. YES, PUN INTENDED

1

- Begin by rendering down your bacon (1 lb.) in a ceramic lined cast iron pot/Dutch oven on medium low.
- This will take approximately **15 - 20 minutes** as you'll have to do it in 2 batches. The bacon won't all fit in the pot. Remove it from the pot once rendered, & chop into small bites.

The STAR of all Chowders: JUICY POTATOES

2

- 2 large Russet Potatoes – chopped into ½ in.
- 1 Large or 2 medium Onions - diced
- 1 tsp. Thyme – fresh or dried
- 1 tsp. Rosemary – fresh
- 2 Bay leaves
- 1 tsp. Salt
- ½ tsp. Pepper
- Thyme – if fresh, pull the leaves off the stocks – you can chop them a little, but no need.
- Rosemary – dice into very small bits. You'll know it's diced enough when you smell it.
- 2 Garlic Cloves – minced or grated

- Chop the potatoes into ½ in. pieces.
- Dice the onions – medium dice works. You don't want the onions to completely disappear.
- Drop in your thyme & chopped rosemary along with chopped or grated garlic & 2 bay leaves.
- Sprinkle in your salt & pepper with a small splash of chicken stock or water to get everything going.
- Cook the **JUICY POTATOES** on medium low for about **10 minutes** adding splashes of stock or water when needed.

3

Time to add:

- 2 large or 3 small carrots - chopped
- 2 celery stocks – chopped
- Cook it all together for another **5 minutes**.
- Then add in 2 – 3 Qtrs. Chicken stock – or the stock of your choice

While the base is simmering, put together your tender meatballs.

MEATBALL MIX:

- 1 Cup of Breadcrumbs, stale bread or panko breadcrumbs – I prefer panko.
- ½ Cup Whole Milk
- 1 Cup Parmesan cheese - grated
- ¼ tsp garlic – granulated or fresh
- ½ tsp oregano
- 1 Tbsp. salt
- ½ Tbsp. Pepper

MEATBALL MEAT:

- ½ lb. Ground turkey – I recommend lean since you are also using pork.
- ½ lb. ground pork – 80/20 works great unless you want it leaner.

NOTE – Always remove protein from the fridge 20 – 30 minutes prior to handling/cooking it. Meat should be room temperature – NOT cold – no matter what type of meat you are using.

CHECK OUT THESE BABIES...

GOBBLE GOBBLE GOES ON A DATE WITH OINK-OINK.

CUTE!

4

- Mix all the meatball ingredients together in a large bowl with your hands, or a large spoon if you prefer.

***Be sure not to over mix. If you do, the meatballs will turn out tough instead of nice & supple.**

5

It's time to roll on & form the meatballs – no pun intended – or was it!

- You can roll the balls with just your hands, or you can use a small ice cream scoop to be sure they are all the same size.

NOTE – rolling the balls is much simpler if you run your hands under cold water first. The meat mixture won't stick to your hands nearly as much.

6

- Place them on a foil lined sheet pan while you are waiting on the base – as pictured aside.

NOTE – You can roast the meatballs at 400 for 10 – 15 minutes if you would like, but I think they turn out better, by just dropping them into the Chowder after you've added stock. You won't believe how tender these meatballs turn out after cooking in the Chowder.

- Due to lining the sheet pan with foil, until you're ready to drop the meatballs into the pot, all the clean-up you have is to remove the foil from the pan & throw it away.

7
- When the base comes to a simmer, put in your chopped, rendered bacon & lightly drop in the meatballs.
- If you aren't comfortable using your hands due to the heat/steam, use a large spoon & lower the balls into the Chowder.

NOTE – Whatever you do, DON'T plop the meatballs into the pot of Chowder high above the pot. If you do, there is a good chance the Chowder will splatter & burn you – let's avoid that! Lightly drop them in by hand or use a large spoon.

8
- When everything has simmered together with a lid on (ajar), for **45 minutes**, taste for seasoning & texture.
- Should it be too thin for your taste, take the lid off & simmer for another **15 minutes**, or until you are happy with the texture.
- Bring it all home - pour in ½ - 1 C. half & half or heavy cream – OFF the heat.
- I like a grating of Parmesan cheese on my bowl, but it's not necessary.

MINI MEATBALLS SUBMERGED IN DELICIOUS CHOWDER.

THIS IS A STICK TO YOUR RIBS BOWL OF FOOD!

CHICKEN PORK EATBALL *Shake Ups*

1. *Chicken Meatball Quesadillas*
2. *Chicken Meatball Sandwich*
3. *Chicken Meatball Chowder Over Polenta*

CHICKEN MEATBALL QUESADILLAS

It's time to put on some music & shake-it-up while you make some quesadillas!

HIGHLIGHTS

No need to go out for Quesadillas.

Enjoy them at home on the cheap!

The Meatball Chowder itself is so luxurious, it takes practically nothing to turn it into a wonderful Quesadilla.
This is how simple it is.

1
- Warm your Chowder in a small saucepan. Two C. will be plenty for 4 large Quesadillas.
- Once you cut the quesadillas into 4 triangular segments (as you would see in any restaurant), the result is 16 pieces.

2
- When the Chowder is warmed through, add approximately 1 C. of shredded cheese.
- For Quesadillas, my preference is Pepper Jack, but you can use Monterey Jack, or sharp cheddar if you don't enjoy spice.
- Guess what, we're pretty much there.

Let's talk flour tortillas...

3
- Warm the flour tortillas over an open flame for **5 seconds** a side.
- Use thongs to turn them so you don't burn yourself.
- Or for an electric stove, put them in a hot, dry skillet and warm the tortillas that way.
- It takes about **a minute** a side to warm & become pliable.

If you want to ERR on the side of caution, just soften them in the microwave between moistened paper towels for 10 seconds.

ALREADY, I CAN SEE THE GOAL LINE!

STEPS — *I TEND TO GET AHEAD OF MYSELF SOMETIMES*

HERE'S INNING #1

1

- Using a slotted spoon, strain out some of the meatballs from the Chowder & chop into halves or quarters. It is great if you also have some of the vegetables from the base included as well. The vegetables will add flavor and some texture to the dish.
- Warm Chowder with the cut meatballs in a saucepan on low.
- All in all, you want around 1 ½ C. of meatballs & jus from the Chowder to make 4 – 6 servings. You can always add if you need/want more filling for the quesadillas.
- With this quesadilla, I chose to add some fresh sweet corn, – 2 or 3 ears is great. There is something about chicken & corn together – it just works.
- While the Chowder is warming, make some crème. This is all it takes...
- Mix ½ C. Greek yogurt or sour cream with the juice of a lime and a pinch of salt & pepper. If it's a little thick, add a few drops of water, or even better, a small amount of stock for extra flavor.

Time to start on the tortillas...

2

- If you have a gas stove, all you need to do is sear them directly on the open flame, using thongs. It will take only **5 seconds** per side until the tortillas are warmed & blistered a bit. Should you have an electric range, put the dry tortillas in a pan on high heat – one at a time – until they start to bubble. Either way you heat the tortillas, once they are done, stack them in paper towels until you are ready to build the quesadillas.

Time for, in my opinion, the best part – CHEESE!

3

- Grate about 1 C. cheese to glue everything together. You can use any combination of the following: Sharp Cheddar, Grated Mozzarella or Provolone, or a combination of both – the kind you get in bags at the grocery store, Fontina, or Gouda. ***If you use a block of cheese instead of already grated cheese, thinly slicing it can be quicker & easier - Just a tip***

Bring on some awesome quesadillas...

4

- Take the warmed flour tortillas and put them on a large sheet pan to easily build the layers.
- First on the tortilla goes a layer or cheese.
- Second is the warmed meatball Chowder with fresh corn.
- Third is another layer of cheese – to glue it all together as I mentioned above.
- Finish by putting them into a **350 oven for 8 minutes** - warm and melt the cheese.
- Alternatively, you can put them into a skillet on the top of your stove covered with a lid or some foil, until the cheese starts to melt. Get ready for chicken meatball, **cheesy goodness**
- Once plated, dollop the quesadillas with your crème and your favorite salsa or Pico.

WHAT A SATISFYING LUNCH OR DINNER.

IT'S BURSTING WITH FLAVOR!

PARMIGIANA SANDWICHES

IF YOU ENJOY MEATBALL PARMIGIANA SUBS,
THIS ONE IS CERTAINLY FOR YOU!

Meatball Parmigiana Subs, or simply called, Meatball Parm Subs are on almost every Italian American restaurant menu. ***What a great Shake-Up.*** *You have a combo of Chicken Parm & Meatball Parm all in one!*

STEPS

1

- First things first – using a slotted spoon, remove some of the meatballs from the Chowder & put them into a small saucepan

2

- To the meatballs, add about ½ C. of your own homemade marinara, or even easier, your favorite jarred tomato sauce from the grocery.
- Let the meatballs and sauce warm on low heat with a slanted lid (partially covered).
- If the sauce begins to spit at you, turn it off. It's easy to warm it back up when toasting the rolls.

Speaking of rolls.

- The worst thing you can do to a Parm Sandwich (any kind – meatball, chicken, eggplant), is to put it on a hard, tough roll.
- Biting through it will result in a mess and unfortunately, you'll end up with more than half the meatballs & cheese on the plate and a hard, plain roll in your hands.

A fresh soft roll is imperative here!

3

- Cut your rolls lengthwise down the middle, being sure not to cut all the way through. Leave a bare minimum of 1 in. thickness on the bottom of the roll.
- That way, the sauce and filling will not leak though the bread.

SOFT ROLL DRIZZLED WITH OLIVE OIL ALONGSIDE SLICED FRESH MOZZARELLA & GRATED PARMIGIANA.

4
- Drizzle the cut rolls with some olive oil and toast them on a foil lined sheet pan, in the oven for **5 minutes** on **350**.
- You're just looking for a little crispiness on the outside of the roll. They will crisp more once they go back into the oven to melt the cheese on top, after the sandwich is built.

Speaking of cheese.

5
- Slice some fresh mozzarella into ¼ in. pieces. You'll need about 3 slices per sandwich – of course, depending on the size of the soft roll you are using.
- You can also use a packaged grated mozzarella if that is more convenient

6
- It's time to grate some Parmesan cheese. Parmigiano Reggiano is the absolute best – always!
- You'll need approximately ½ C. of grated Parm cheese to top four good size subs.

It's always best to use the freshest of cheeses, but these days, the packaged combination of grated Italian cheeses won't hurt this dish – just get the best brand you can

7
- After your rolls are lightly toasted and out of the oven, drop in the saucy meatballs and top with the mozzarella & Parm.

8
- Put the sandwiches back onto the foil lined sheet pan & bake at 350 until the cheese is melted. It will take approximately **5 -10 minutes**.

Between the tender meatballs, marinara, gooey cheese & toasted buns, you'll never order out for one of these again.

WELL, NOT NEARLY AS OFTEN AT LEAST!

Ch & Shake-Ups

MEATBALL CHOWDER OVER POLENTA

Silky Polenta topped with tender meatballs & veg from the Chowder.

IT TASTES LAVISH, BUT IN ALL REALITY, IT'S SIMPLE RUSTIC FOOD.

You can go out & pay OH, about $18 for meatball polenta or you can make this Shake-Up for your loved ones at home & save your hard-earned bucks.

You'll have this dish done for your family & friends in 10 minutes.

Polenta is a cheap, quick & delicious side dish for any protein – chicken, beef, pork, fish or even beans.

It's all good!

STEPS

1

- For the Polenta, follow the package directions. With that said, in my opinion, a good ratio of liquid to corn meal is
- 4 to 1 (4 parts liquid to 1-part corn meal.) As for the liquid, see the note below.

****Note – many use water to make their polenta. I think that's a big mistake. Anytime you can add more flavor to a dish – DO IT!***

- Instead of water, use ½ portion Stock (Chicken or Vegetable), & ½ portion whole milk or half & half. Also, be sure to warm your liquids. Don't add the corn meal to cold liquid.

CHOWDER CORNMEAL & MEATBALLS

This rolls out in about ***10 minutes***.

2

- When you are adding the corn meal to the warm pool, whisk rapidly until you see the polenta set up. It will take **2 minutes**, MAX.
- Turn down the heat as soon as it starts to create bubbles. Otherwise, it can spit out of the pot & burn you.

3

- Lastly add a ¼ C. grated Parmigiana Reggiano & 2 TBSP. of butter. Whisk it all together.
- Give it a taste for salt & pepper & adjust to your palate.
- Put a lid or some foil on top of the saucepan, to keep it warm while the Chowder is heating.

POLENTA, MEATBALL LUXURY ABOUT TO HAPPEN.

4
- Now that the polenta is done, warm your Chowder in a small saucepan on low, as usual. Depending on how many servings you are preparing, a good guideline would be about 2 C. of Chowder per 4 servings.
- This way you have enough meatballs.
- When the Chowder is warm, all that remains is to plate the dish

5
- Spoon the creamy polenta onto a plate or into a bowl & top with your Meatball Chowder.

A KNIFE OR FORK ISN'T NEEDED FOR THIS MEAL - *JUST A SPOON!*

LASAGNA CHOWDER

NOT 1 BUT 2 WAYS.

Take your pick.

red or white sauce (with a little green),

if you like pesto.

LASAGNA CHOWDER- *Classic Red*

THE LONG & SHORT OF IT IS JUST THIS...

To the Chowder Base, ADD a can of tomatoes, some ricotta cheese & pasta
See measurements below.

STEPS

1

- In the pot of the **JUICY POTATOES** & the rest of the base, pour in a 28 oz. can of good **San Marzano tomatoes** & 1 Qt. of chicken stock.
- Put the heat on medium low – you're looking for a low simmer. It will be about **10 minutes** until the tomatoes, **JUICY POTATOES** & base, simmer down & come together (thicken a bit).

NOTE – Please season with salt & pepper every single time you add any ingredient to the dish.

- With that said, it's time to taste & even out the flavors. You might want another sprinkling of salt & or some pepper.
- There's also nothing wrong with a dash of cayenne or your favorite hot sauce if you like a little kick

2

- Now it's time to bring a pot of water to a boil. Once it comes to a boil, throw in a good amount of salt – taste it once it dissolves, it should taste like the sea.
- Into the boiling salted water, add your short pasta, i.e., elbows, cavatappi, fusilli.

NOTE – It's essential that you cook the pasta for this dish, half of the package directions.

- Once the pasta is mixed in with the Chowder, it will continue to cook. I can't say it enough, overcooked pasta is a cook's disaster!

3

- Drain the pasta & set aside for **a minute** while the remainder of the dish comes together.
- At this point, you should be happy with the flavor & texture of the Chowder.

4

- Turn the heat down to low – as low as your stove gets. The dairy that you are going to include, will separate if the heat is too high.

5

- ¼ C. Half & Half or Heavy Cream
- ½ C. Good Ricotta cheese – this is not the place to go light. For the number of portions, you are making, use the full fat.
- Stir it all together. Give it a taste & if it's tickling your palate, move onto the last couple ingredients...Your cooked rested pasta
- ¼ lb. chopped fresh mozzarella
- Finish with a grating of salty/tangy Parmesan cheese – how much is up to you.

WHERE'S YOUR SPOON?

LASAGNA CHOWDER #2

Great way to utilize the classic **LASAGNA CHOWDER** with addition of Pesto.
It turns into a completely different dish.
As you can see, I used leftover pizza crust for a nice dipper. It works out very well.
I think you'll approve!

JUST A FEW DIFFERENCES BETWEEN LASAGNA CHOWDER #1 & #2

STEPS *differences listed here*

1 Use half the number of canned tomatoes. Instead of a 28 oz. can use a 14 oz. can.

2 Add an extra ¼ C. ricotta cheese.

If the Chowder starts to get a little too thick for your liking, do what I always say, splash in some extra stock until it's at the consistency you desire.

3 **PESTO** - The final difference in this Chowder. You can make it yourself if you want, but store bought today is of great quality.

Stir in ¼ C. & your Chowder is finished.

I like to make this Chowder Brulé style by topping it with mozzarella & parmesan cheese. Put in your oven under the broiler to melt the cheese, but if you don't want the extra cheese, it's just as tasty without it.

THERE YOU HAVE IT, TWO LASAGNA CHOWDERS THAT COULDN'T BE EASIER TO PREPARE.

IF YOU'RE A "LASAGNA NIGHT" FAMILY,

wait until you grace your table with bowls of this CHOWDER!

LASAGNA *Shake Ups*

1. Lasagna Balls
2. Lasagna Egg Scramble
3. Lasagna Burrito

LASAGNA BALLS

**SOUNDS FUNNY I KNOW. BUT BELIEVE ME,
YOU'VE NEVER HAD A "MEATBALL" LIKE THIS!**

STEPS

This recipe will create 16 - 20 Lasagna Balls.

1
- **Preheat your oven to 400.**
- Reduce 2 C. Lasagna Chowder on low for about **10 minutes**, or until all the jus has dissipated

2
- Mix together your reduced Chowder, ½ C. Panko & ½ C. grated Parmigiana cheese.

3
- Line a baking sheet with foil & brush on some olive oil so that the meatballs will come off the pan easily

4
- Roll them out baby. I roll them with my hands but using a small ice cream scoop works very well. That way you know they will all be the same size & bake evenly.

There's nothing wrong with a domed "Meatball" - tastes just as good.

5
- Bake the meatballs for **15 minutes**.
- Let them rest for at least **5 – 10 minutes**.

I like a fresh & easy side with these decadent meatballs. All I did is drizzle some fresh green beans with a little olive oil & sprinkle them with a pinch of salt & pepper.

- Toss them in a bowl & **DONE** – no cooking needed!

Let's play ball!

As you can see below, the meatballs will flatten a little while they are baking.
That's due to the marinara in the Chowder.
Marinara in these balls, enhance the flavor.
Lasagna & meatballs all in one bite - sweet!
These will be the supplest meatballs you've ever had!
Pull these "Meatballs" together···

LASAGNA IN THE FORM OF A "MEATBALL"

What's next?

A hotdog topped with caviar?

LASAGNA EGG SCRAMBLE

Scrambled Eggs with Lasagna Chowder.
Takes 5 minutes – Directions next

STEPS

There are very few steps to this Shake-Up

1

- For 4 6 servings, warm Lasagna Chowder (1 C.) in a saucepan on low - due to the thickness, it can easily spit at you. It only needs to reduce for about **5 - 10 minutes**.

2

- Separately, in a large bowl, whisk your eggs. Typically, 2 eggs per person is sufficient.
- The addition of Chowder bulks up the dish. Due to all the flavors in the Chowder itself, you don't even need to season the eggs.

You'll know the Chowder is reduced when your spatula creates separation in your pan

3

- In a large sauté pan on low, drizzled with about 1 Tbsp. olive oil, add the whisked eggs & warmed Chowder.
- Using a spatula, stir the eggs & Chowder together until the eggs coagulate.
- I enjoy my eggs on the softer side (which would take about **5 minutes**) but cook them to your preferred consistency.
- As far as the side for this dish, you can't go wrong with some Olive Oil Garlic Toast.

DOESN'T GET EASIER THAN THAT!

LASAGNA BURRITO

PATH TO BURRITO TOWN.

STEPS

1
- Warm the Chowder in a saucepan on low until it's just that, warm & somewhat condensed – **10 minutes**.

2
- Using flour tortillas warm them in a 375 oven for **5 minutes** or on the top of your gas stove.
- Using thongs to flip the tortillas, it takes 5 seconds per side for the tortillas to become soft & supple.
- Stack the tortillas together so they remain warm.
- Building the burritos is all that's between you & a handheld wonderful meal…

3
- Put a layer of cheese – Cheddar, Monterey Jack, Fontina, American - on the warm tortillas & then spoon on your Chowder.
- Wrap the burritos & serve with Pico or your favorite salsa & some crema or some good Greek yogurt.

***If this is a to-go meal, you can drizzle the Pico/salsa & crema inside the burrito – just be sure to wrap it tightly with foil or parchment paper so it doesn't get messy.**

THAT'S ALL SHE WROTE!

HOT AND SOUR CHOWDER

IF YOU LIKE ASIAN FLAVORS,
THIS CHOWDER IS CERTAINLY FOR YOU.
IT'S SALTY, HOT & TANGY, IT'S CREAMY.
IT'S FILLED WITH VEGGIES

BETTER THAN YOUR TAKEAWAY HOT & SOUR SOUP!

INGREDIENTS

BASE

- 1 lb. of Bacon

JUICY POTATOES

- 1 Large or 2 medium Onions
- 3 Large Russet Potatoes
- 1 tsp. Thyme – fresh or dried
- 1 tsp. Rosemary – fresh
- 2 Bay leaves – fresh or dried
- ½ tsp. Salt
- ¼ tsp. Pepper

- 3 Small or 2 medium Carrots
- 3 Celery Stocks
- 2 Garlic Cloves

Here is where the Hot & Sour comes to the playground

Marinade for the protein:

- 2 Tbsp. Rice Vinegar
- 2 Tbsp. Toasted Sesame Seed Oil
- 2 Tbsp. Cornstarch

STEPS

1

- Cut 1 lb. boneless skinless chicken thighs or pork loin (whatever meat you chose), into ¼ inch pieces.
- Add the protein, vinegar, sesame seed oil & cornstarch into a storage bag and let marinade in the fridge for at least **30 minutes**.
- No longer than an hour, due to the vinegar – it will break down the meat too much. When your protein is marinated, next is to simply incorporate everything together.

2

- To the BASE, marinated meat and 3 to 4 quarts chicken stock (start with 3), add the following:
- 2 TBSP of grated ginger
- 4 cloves of garlic – grated or minced
- ¼ cup soy sauce – you could use shoyu or liquid aminos if you prefer.
- ¾ cup rice vinegar
- 1 Tbsp. Sambal Oelek – International Isle in your grocery story or online. You can also substitute with 1 tsp. Chili Flakes.
- 4 – 6 oz. Shitake &/or Cremini mushrooms– sliced into quarter/half inch slices.
- 2 large eggs – whisk them in a bowl, then slowly stir into the warm Chowder so that it turns into thin ribbons. You don't want to whisk eggs once you put them into the Chowder – just lightly stir them in.

3

- Finish with a ¼ C. of heavy cream or half & half. Be sure the Chowder is off the heat when adding dairy otherwise it may curdle

YOUR SALIVARY GLANDS ARE ABOUT TO THANK YOU!

HOT & SOUR *Shake Ups*

1. *Hot & Sour Tuna Salad with Egg Noodles*
2. *Hot & Sour Wings*
3. *A Take on Hot & Sour Hervos Rancheros*

HOT & SOUR TUNA SALAD WITH EGG NOODLES

Coming your way – another easy Shake-Up.
Hot & sour tuna salad with egg noodles
You can prepare this dish with one hand behind your back.

THIS IS NOT YOUR GRANDMOTHER'S TUNA CASSEROLE!

STEPS

1
- Take 1 ½ C. of your Chowder & warm it in a medium sized saucepan on low with two 5 oz. cans of tuna packed in olive oil. A good size saucepan is perfect as the dish will all be finished in that same pan.

2
- While the Chowder is warming, take a 2 Qt. saucepan & fill it ¾ of the way with cold water.
- Cover the pot with a lid and bring to a boil on high heat. Once the water comes to a boil, salt it liberally – it will be more salt than you think. Don't be afraid to taste the water itself. It should taste like the sea. If it doesn't, add more.
- For this dish, I used longer egg noodles, but if you want to use the old school bagged egg noodles, that ke- out just as well. When your water is boiling and salted, add the noodles.
- You'll need approximately ½ C. of pasta for each portion – depending on how small or large a portion you & your family want, regardless.
- Always undercook your pasta **2 minutes** short of the package directions. The pasta will continue to cook once you add it together with the tuna & Chowder mixture.

- Pour your drained pasta into the saucepan of warmed Chowder & tuna - stir it all together
- I like the addition of frozen peas for a sweet touch & texture – a ¼ C. should suffice. You can incorporate them right at the end. The warm Chowder mixture will defrost them in a minute – plus it will stop the pasta from overcooking.
- After everything is tossed together & plated or bowled, drizzle with a tiny bit of Extra Virgin olive oil.
- This last step is controversial – to cheese or not to cheese. I like a topping of grated Parmigiana cheese here. It's your call – don't be ashamed if you enjoy tuna & cheese together.

Come on, tell me you don't want to defy the norm & put some cheese in your tuna noodle dish! Plus, who doesn't love a good tuna melt time to time?

HOT & SOUR WINGS

THERE IS NO NEED TO FRY WINGS.
Baked wings are just as delicious and believe it or not, just as crispy.

SO CUTE FOR A COCKTAIL PARTY!
HAVE YOUR WING AND SAUCE IN ONE RAMEKIN.
EVERYONE GETS THEIR OWN. FUN!

Takeaway – NOPE. Veer away from the Buffalo sauce & Shake It Up with these Sticky & Spicy Wings.

STEPS

If you haven't baked chicken wings, please give it a go. It's easy & believe it or not, they are just as crispy as the fried version we all know.

1

- **Preheat your oven to 450** & line a large baking sheet with foil & about **1 TBSP**. or so of a light oil - canola, safflower, sunflower.

If you have a wire rack that sits on top of your baking sheet, use it here. It allows the fat to fall to the bottom of the sheet pan, so the wings aren't sitting in the fat as they roast.

- Be sure to brush the rack with oil so the wings won't stick. Due to the sugar in the sauce of these wings, they can easily stick.

2

- Using a large spoon, take out about ½ C. of your Hot & Sour Chowder - leaving behind the solids.

If you end up with a few pieces of veg, that's fine – just not too much, otherwise your sauce won't glaze the wings as easily.

3

- Warm the Chowder sauce in a small saucepan on low.

BRING IT HOME WITH COMBINING THE FOLLOWING TO YOUR CHOWDER:

- 2 TBSP. Tamari or Soy sauce
- **2 TBSP Brown sugar** - light or dark works
- **1 TBSP Sambal Oelek, 2 TBSP. Sweet Chili Sauce** - these are ingredients you'll find in the international aisle of your grocery store or online. If you can't find sweet chili sauce, use **1 TBSP. of apricot preserves** for sweetness & thickness. This will help make a beautiful glaze that will stick to the wings. If you are not familiar with Sambal Oelek, all it is a ground chili paste.
- Should you not be able to find it, use **¼ tsp. dried chili flakes** mixed with **2 tsp. fresh lemon or lime juice OR even better,** a small dash **(1 TBSP.) of balsamic vinegar**. It has a nice sweetness that helps thicken the sauce as well.

4 ⅋ Allow all ingredients along with the Chowder sauce reduce on low until you see it thicken. You'll know it's ready when it coats the back of a wooden or plastic spoon. Of course, taste to ensure that it's evenly seasoned. ***The flavors should be a level combination of heat, sour, salty & sweet.***

⅋ Now for the wings themselves. If you are making whole wings, i.e., the drumette, flat wingette & tip all still together, they will take about **45 minutes** to roast. On the other hand, if your wings are cut into drumettes & wingettes, it will only take about **35 minutes** to roast.

⅋ Clearly, the roasting time all depends on the size of your wings, but what I mentioned above is a good guideline. You won't go wrong!

⅋ Salt and Pepper, the wings - not too much salt, as the sauce has plenty in it already.

5 ⅋ Lay the wings on your oil lined sheet pan or on an oiled wire rack and roast for **25 minutes**.

6 ⅋ After **25 minutes** take them out of the oven & brush liberally with your reduced sauce. Put the wings back into the oven & roast them for **10 more minutes** - or longer if your wings are huge.

IT'S BEYOND WORTH IT!!

7 ⅋ Once the wings are finished roasting, remove from the oven & let them rest - see tip below. **A BIG tip here is to let the wings rest for 5 or 10 minutes** - especially if you are using a wire rack. The wings will release from the rack so much easier after sitting a few.

If you placed them directly on the foil lined sheet pan using thongs, take them off the pan right when they come out of the oven and blot the bottom of the wings on paper towels to remove some of the fat – only the bottom, you don't want to mess with the delicious sticky sauce you made on the top.

⅋ After letting them sit, put the wings in a large bowl & spoon on more sauce. Toss them so that the sauce is evenly coated all over the wings.

⅋ Plate these babies up and go for it. You'll be covered in the scrumptious glaze, but let' s be honest.

WHAT A FUN WEEKNIGHT OR WEEKEND DINNER WITH FAMILY & FRIENDS!

HOT & SOUR HUEVOS RANCHEROS

IF YOU ENJOY HUEVOS RANCHEROS, THIS IS A NICE TWIST ON THAT DISH!
IT IS ALSO A VERY TASTY GLUTEN FREE MEAL.

STEPS

1

- Open a can of refried beans & warm on low in a small saucepan. You'll need to thin out the beans a bit with some stock or even water – a few dashes should be enough. You want it to be pourable because when it hits the plate, it sets up quickly.

As for the eggs/Chowder part of the dish, check it out below:

2

- For 4 – 6 servings, in a large bowl, whisk together 6 eggs with ½ C. of your Chowder.
- You do not need to drain much of the JUS from the Chowder in this instance.
- A little of the liquid added to the eggs, results in a surprisingly supple texture. If you prefer your eggs well done, that's no big whoop.

3

- Cook eggs in your sauté pan with 2 Tbsp. Olive Oil or Butter until you achieve your desired texture.
- Stir with a spatula regularly so the eggs & Chowder do **NOT** brown or even worse, burn.
- No matter how you like your eggs, it won't take more than **10 minutes** on low – I accentuate **LOW!**

Eggs should never be cooked on high heat – they'll end up tough.

- When it comes to the toppings, use whatever you enjoy on most Mexican/South American dishes.
- As you can see in the photos, I like the crunch of some almonds, the tangy spiciness of hot pepper rings & the brightness of a sprinkling of cilantro.
- Grated cheese is never a bad idea either.
- Salsa & or Pico de Gallo bring freshness as well.

THIS DISH IS HEALTHFUL, BEAUTIFUL & A CINCH TO PULL TOGETHER.

NOT TO MENTION EASY ON THE POCKET!

SPINACH ARTICHOKE CHOWDER

INGREDIENTS

BASE/DNA

- 1 lb. of Bacon

JUICY POTATOES

- 3 Large Russet Potatoes
- 1 Large or 2 medium Onions
- 2 Tbsp. Butter or Olive Oil – or a combination.
- 2 Bay leaves
- 1 Tbsp. Salt
- ½ Tbsp. Pepper
- 1 tsp. Thyme – fresh or dried
- 1 tsp. Rosemary – fresh
- Splashes of Stock or Water – about ¼ - ½ C.

REMAINING INGREDIENTS

- 2 medium Carrots
- 2 Celery Stocks
- 2 Garlic Cloves
- 2 Cans Artichoke Hearts – drained
- 1 lb. Frozen Spinach
- 8 oz. Cream Cheese
- ½ C. Grated Parmesan
- ½ C. Half & Half or Heavy Cream

STEPS

1

- Begin by rendering down your bacon (1 lb.) in a ceramic lined cast iron pot/Dutch oven on medium low.
- This will take approximately **15 - 20 minutes** as you'll have to do it in 2 batches. The bacon won't all fit in the pot.
- Remove it from the pot once rendered, & chop into small bites.

2

- Chop the potatoes into ½ in. pieces.
- Dice the onions – medium dice works. You don't want the onions to completely disappear.
- Drop in your thyme & chopped rosemary along with chopped or grated garlic & 2 bay leaves.
- Sprinkle in your salt & pepper with a small splash of chicken stock or water to get everything going.
- Cook the **JUICY POTATOES** on medium low for about **10 minutes** adding splashes of stock or water when needed.

3

Time to add:

- 2 large or 3 small carrots - chopped
- 2 celery stocks - chopped
- Cook it all together for another **5 minutes** then add in
- 2 – 3 Qt. Chicken stock – or the stock of your choice.
- 2x 15 oz. Cans of Artichokes – drained
- 1 lb. Pack of Frozen Spinach – defrosted & all water squeezed out using a kitchen towel.

4

- Put the lid on your pot ajar & let simmer on medium low for **30 minutes.**

5

- Add in 8 oz. Cream Cheese
- ½ C. Grated Parmesan Cheese

DON'T GET EASIER THAT *MANGIA!*

SPINACH ARTICHOKE *Shake Ups*

1. Spinach Artichoke Pizza
2. Spinach Artichoke Beef & Chicken Roll-Ups
3. Spinach Artichoke Stuffed Tomatoes

SPINACH ARTICHOKE PIZZA

To make this an extra speedy meal, I believe in refrigerated pizza dough from the grocery store. They are quite good these days.

STEPS

1
- **Preheat your oven to 425**.
- Take the dough out of the refrigerator about an hour before making the pizza. You can also take the dough out when you leave for work in the morning. It will be ready to work with when you get home.

2
- Warm the Chowder (1 ½ C.) in a small saucepan on low to cook down and reduce (about **10 – 15 minutes**), – nothing different from most of the *SHAKE-UP* recipes.
- Always stir every **3 or so minutes** so the starch doesn't stick on the bottom of the pan.

3
- Roll the pizza dough out to the thinness/thickness of your liking on a lightly floured surface. The crust will puff up and expand as it bakes, so it's best to roll the dough out a bit on the thinner side.
- Lightly coat/brush the rolled-out dough on both sides, with extra virgin olive oil.

4
- After transferring the dough to your ½ Sheet Pan, season the top of the dough with salt and pepper.

5
- Bake the dough as it is (no toppings yet), at 425 for **10 minutes**.
- After **10 minutes**, it should look like the pizza crust we all know and love - golden with bubbles starting to form. At this point your Chowder should be nicely reduced.

6
- To the Chowder add 2 -3 Tbsp. of cream cheese or crème fraiche and stir together until incorporated.
- Once the pizza crust is out of the oven, spoon on a layer of the Chowder mixture and spread it out to all edges of the crust.
- Put as much sauce on the pizza as you would like. You can't go wrong. **This is an AMAZING "white pizza" sauce!**

STRAIGHT OUT OF THE OVEN – BEFORE A SPRINKLING OF BASIL

WHAT A SHAKE-UP SPINACH ARTICHOKE DIP & PIZZA!

7
- Top the pizza with your choice of cheeses. I like fresh mozzarella and Parmigiano Reggiano, but you can use a store-bought mix of bagged cheeses for ease.

8
- Put the pizza back into the oven to melt the cheese. It should only take **5 – 7 minutes**, depending on the cheese you are using.
- You don't want the crust to get too browned & crispy, so give it a peek after **5 minutes**. If the cheese is melted, it's done. Remember that the crust is already baked through, so melting the cheese is all we're doing.
- I say WE, because I wish I was with you when making this fantastic *SHAKE-UP*.

DON'T PICK UP THE PHONE FOR TAKEAWAY.

THIS PIZZA ROCKS!

SPINACH ARTICHOKE ROLL-UPS

ROLL IT UP – LITTLE DARLING!

Bet you never thought of making a roll-up from some leftover Chowder!
Your family will have fun with this easy & tasty Shake-Up!

STEPS

Once you thinly slice the chicken & beef & sauté it in a skillet, it should remind you of the meat you get on a cheesesteak – golden brown

1

- Warm 1 C. of the Chowder in a pan on low. You want the Chowder to reduce a little so that it resembles more of a sauce than a Chowder. This should take about **10 minutes**.

2

- When it comes to the meat, you can thinly slice a couple chicken breasts & a small steak. The best cut of steak would be ribeye, but it tends to be pricey.
- Another route that would be cheaper is skirt steak or top sirloin. You don't need much beef here (½ lb.) as the chicken & Chowder fill in the gaps.

****NOTE – There is also nothing wrong with purchasing sliced roast beef from your deli section. It's much cheaper & it sears in your pan in seconds.***

3

- As always, **NEVER** forget to season your meat with salt & pepper before you cook it. You can add whatever seasonings you want, but I think granulated onion & granulated garlic are best here.

4

- No matter what you use, cook the meat on high in stir-fry fashion (put it in the pan with a little oil & move it all around constantly until it's just cooked through.)
- This will take no longer than **2 – 3 minutes** as long as your meat is cut very thin & your heat is on high. Now the flour tortillas. In this preparation, I think utilizing your microwave is the way to go.

5

- All you have to do is moisten a clean kitchen towel or some paper towels. Stack the tortillas between the paper towels on a plate and put them in the microwave for **20 -30 seconds** depending on how many you are warming.
- For 6 large tortillas, **30 seconds** is perfect. If you're only warming 4, leave it at **20 seconds**.

****NOTE – Don't remove the kitchen towel/paper towels until you are ready to wrap & roll***

6
- Take a warm tortilla, spread on some of your reduced Chowder.
- Top the Chowder with seared chicken & beef. Feel free to add some cheese if you'd like, but I think the Chowder is cheesy & creamy enough.
- Guacamole or just sliced avocado would rock here too.

Wrap & roll it all together.

7
- Cut it into pieces if you want (like above) or eat it burrito style.
- I chose to accompany this with a simple tomato corn salad since it was in season, but any side salad would be nice (easy green salad, potato salad, macaroni salad, etc.).
- Another thing you can pick up at the store if you don't want to spend the time/have the time to make it.

A flavor filled meal that will take less than 30 minutes to put together.

WHY CHOOSE WHEN YOU CAN HAVE IT ALL – CHICKEN, BEEF & SPINACH ARTICHOKE ALL IN ONE WRAP?

BRING IT!

SPINACH ARTICHOKE STUFFED TOMATOES

Think spinach artichoke dip engulfed in a seasoned tomato. SWEET!
Making these beautiful and yummy stuffed tomatoes is a snap.
They'll be made and baked in about 30 minutes – maybe less

STEPS

Here comes my usual repeat...

1

- **Preheat your oven to 375**.
- Reduce the Chowder in a small saucepan on low. For these stuffed tomatoes, you'll need about 1 C. of the Chowder. Remember to use a slotted spoon.
- While the Chowder is reducing, it's time to take on the tomatoes. I find that the best type of tomatoes to use for this recipe are Campari & Beefsteak, but feel free to use whatever tomato your market has that looks good.

One more note on the tomatoes, no matter what type you use, be sure that they are not overly ripe.

- You want a sturdy tomato in order to stuff and roast it properly.

2

- Using a spoon or a butter knife, remove the seeds and ribs of the tomatoes so you have an empty tomato to stuff.
- Once you have the inside of the tomato cleared out, season the inside with salt and pepper.

3

- Put the tomatoes upside down on paper towels so that the liquid can drain. It only takes about **5 minutes**.
- If you skip this step, the rendered Chowder stuffing will end up too wet and the tomato will deflate – **NOT GOOD!**
- Now that the tomatoes are ready and the Chowder is at the end of cooking down, we just need to finish the stuffing and add the topping.

Seeded & seasoned tomatoes, ready for stuffing.
Do NOT forget the seasoning step in this recipe. It's crucial!
If you don't let the tomatoes release some of their liquid, it will not stand up to the filling & you'll end up with flat tires.
NO THANKS!

4
- To the reduced Chowder, add about 3 Tbsp. of Cream cheese & ¼ C. of either grated Parmesan or Pecorino cheese.
- Incorporate ¼ C. Panko breadcrumbs and mix the stuffing all together.
- If for whatever reason the stuffing seems too stiff, just add a few dashes of milk or stock. Be careful to not add too much liquid.
- Between the Chowder and the cheeses, you shouldn't need any extra liquid. Remember that you will also get moisture from the tomato itself.

5
- Stuff the tomatoes with the warm Chowder, cheese & panko mixture & top them with more panko and grated Parmesan cheese – a ½ C. total should be plenty to top 4 – 6 tomatoes.
- Drizzle the top of the stuffed tomatoes with a little extra virgin olive oil or spray.

6
- As for roasting these, I use small glass ramekins so the tomatoes can't roll around in the oven. If you don't have small ramekins, wrap the tomato with a couple layers of foil – keeping the top uncovered so it will brown. This will ensure that the tomatoes don't fall over or roll around. Crumple up some foil to make a "bed" for the tomatoes to sit in/on.

7
- Place the stuffed tomatoes on a foil lined baking sheet and put in the oven at 375 (mentioned above) for **20 – 25 minutes**, or until the topping is golden.
- This really all depends on your oven as everybody's oven works differently.
- These tomatoes are a great light, but comforting weeknight dinner. Pair them with a side salad of your liking and you're done.
- Pictured above with the finished roasted tomatoes, is a simple salad of edamame and grated carrots with a vinaigrette dressing.

Golden baked stuffed tomatoes with a side salad of edamame and carrots. It may not seem it, but this is one COMFORTING DISH!

SOO GOOD!

TOMATO SOUP CHOWDER

INGREDIENTS

BASE/DNA:

- 1 lb. of Bacon

THE INFAMOUS JUICY POTATOES:

- 3 Large Russet Potatoes
- 1 Large or 2 medium Onions
- 1 tbsp. Thyme – fresh or dried
- 1 tbsp. Rosemary – fresh
- 2 Bay leaves
- ½ tbsp. Salt
- ¼ tbsp. Pepper
- 3 Small or 2 medium Carrots
- 3 Celery Stocks
- 2 Garlic Cloves

To the base add:

- 1 28 oz. caned San Marzano tomatoes
- 1 C. Heavy Cream or Half & Half

STEPS

Get ready for the difficult part of this recipe?

1

- Using a handheld immersion blender or a regular blender, zip it all together until the Chowder is smooth.
- This is after all, a Tomato Soup Chowder.
- We all think the same thing when it comes to Tomato Soup - silkiness

TOMATO SOUP *Shake Ups*

1. *Eggs in Purgatory*
2. *Chicken Parm*
3. *Rice-a-Roni*
4. *Bonus – Tomato Chicken Mushroom Stew*

PLATED EGGS IN PURGATORY

Include this into your regular repertoire.
It's a BLD dish – I believe that's the acronym for any meal during the day – **Breakfast, Brunch, Lunch Dinner**.

YOUR CALL – IT'S ALL GOOD!

WITH THE USE OF TOMATO CHOWDER, IT'S A CINCH TO PUT TOGETHER.

DIP YOUR TOAST INTO THE CHOWDER & RUNNY EGGS...

YOU'RE CERTAINLY NOT IN PURGATORY!

CHICKEN PARMIGIANA

Thinking of going out for takeout from your local Italian place?

Why?

This dish will pull together in less than 30 minutes & you know it's all quality ingredients!

HIGHLIGHTS

1 • Warm 1 C. of the Tomato Soup Chowder & 1 C. of your favorite jarred Marinara (or homemade if you have it), in a small saucepan on low. You don't want it to boil – just warm through

2 • Take the chicken breast out of the refrigerator at least **30 minutes** to an hour prior to making this dish.

Recipe, Step-by-Step next.

TIPS

I'M NOT SCOLDING YOU, BUT NEVER cook cold protein right out of the refrigerator – the outside will brown, sear and the inside will be raw. As I noted, take it out at least **30 minutes** prior to cooking it.

STEPS

1 . Dry the chicken on paper towel lined plates, or a plastic cutting board.
****DO NOT use a wooden cutting board - in order to avoid cross contamination. Raw poultry regularly carries bacteria. If some bacteria get into your wooden cutting board, it's very difficult to be sure you've removed it all after cleaning it.***

2 Season the chicken with salt and pepper on both sides. Adding a sprinkling of some granulated garlic doesn't hurt, if you groove with garlic that is. I think it elevates the flavor

3 Cover the rested seasoned chicken with plastic wrap prior to pounding it out. This way, your plastic cutting board won't have raw poultry on it – makes for easier cleanup

4 Pound out the chicken breast a bit with a mallet or the back of a skillet so the thicker side of the breast is even with the thinner side – this will ensure even cooking.

5
- Coat the chicken in a large casserole dish with a couple seasoned (salt & pepper) beaten eggs, and then on another large plate, press the chicken into panko breadcrumbs.

Personally, I think you can skip coating your chicken. But, if you like some extra crunch, feel free to coat in the eggs & panko.

6
- With that said, sear off both sides of your chicken on medium heat until it's cooked through.
- **Three minutes** per side should be perfect. Remember that the chicken is going to continue to cook when it goes under the broiler. Plus, it needs to rest for about **5 minutes** after it comes out of the broiler – **a.k.a. carry over cooking.**

Shortly done...

- Turn your broiler on low to preheat for **a couple minutes**.

7
- Top the cooked chicken in the pan with your warmed Chowder/Marinara. Use as much sauce/Chowder as you like. I like at least a ladle or 2 per breast, but I'm a sauce lover - notice the side ramekin of extra sauce.

Now for the cheese:

8
- Provolone and Parmesan are typical for this dish. Sliced Provolone from your deli department works great – that way you don't have to grate it. As for the Parm cheese, it's **ALWAYS** best to grate it yourself – the fresher the better.
- A ¼ C. of sliced provolone & 2 C. of grated Parmesan should work out well for 3 to 4 chicken breasts.
- Lay the sliced Provolone onto the chicken & Chowder, then top it with all that delicious Parmesan.

It's called Chicken Parmesan or Parmigiana (take your pick) for a reason.

9
- Put your pan under the broiler until the cheese starts to brown on top – about **2 minutes** - see pictures above.

A couple side notes:

- Be sure that your pan is ovenproof.
- If you are making many chicken breasts (say 4 or more), it's much easier to roast the meat on sheet pans in the oven – you can use 2 sheet pans if needed. It will take **15 minutes at 400**.
- Once you remove the chicken from the oven, do exactly as mentioned above – top with the Chowder and cheese. Place under the broiler until golden.
- Serve with a simple side salad, baked French fries (from your freezer section), or a side of pasta. Whichever is accustomed to your family.

We have crossed the finish line.

Wasn't that a cinch?

NOTES

Should you not want to take the few minutes to make the chicken breast, stop on the way home from work, or just make a quick run to pick up a rotisserie chicken.
Pull the chicken or just cut it into cubes. When it comes to this dish, remove the skin from the chicken.
Nobody wants fatty skin on their Chicken Parmesan – most don't, I think.

RICE-A-RONI

TOMATO CHOWDER, RICE, RONI, & CHICKEN

A food foursome – Did I just say that

I kid because I LOVE... Food, Family, Fun & Dogs, that is.

GET STARTED. THE RECIPE IS AT YOUR FINGERTIPS.

STEPS

1

- In a large skillet melt a couple Tbsp. of butter and olive oil on low heat.

Don't let the butter brown. When the butter and olive oil get frothy on top, and you can smell what smells like buttered toast, take it off the heat.

2

- Crack your long pasta - "Roni" (spaghetti or linguini) into ¼ in. pieces. The size of pasta doesn't need to be exact at all. Just think of how you would like it to fit on your fork or spoon. Set aside.

3

- Make your long grain rice (Jasmine, Basmati or your favorite long grain rice), HALF the time than the package instructions.
- Stock in my opinion, is better than water for making rice - why not include more flavor.

Cooking the rice half time of the packaged instructions will result in a light fluffy rice. Since the rice is al dente, it will come together nicely with the pasta and Chowder without it over cooking. We're not looking for mushy Rice & Roni!

Now to the skillet of warmed butter and olive oil:

4

- Add your pasta.
- Cook on medium low heat until the pasta turns golden. Toss it around a couple times to be sure it gets golden all over & not just one side. It will take about **3 – 5 minutes** - just keep an eye on it so that it doesn't burn.

5

- Once you see the pasta turn golden and smelling nutty, incorporate the cooked rice to the pan.

6

- Add a few fat splashes (say ¼ C) of stock to the pasta and rice.
- You're just trying to pull both the rice and pasta together to become one.

7

- It's time to add the tomato Chowder & Marinara...
- For 4 portions, 1 C. should be enough to moisten the Rice & Roni. Should you only be making enough for 2 portions, a large ladle of the Chowder & Marinara will be enough.

8 Turn the burner up to high and stir vigorously for **2 minutes**. You'll know that the Rice & Roni is done once the Chowder has cooked down and the Rice & Roni has absorbed the stock and Chowder.

Be sure to not overcook the dish at this point – taste often after you add the Chowder for moisture, texture and flavor.

The finished dish should still be al dente ("to the tooth").

9 **Topping the dish** with some grated hard cheese i.e., Parmesan or Pecorino, is not a bad idea.

Topping the dish with a protein of your choice (chicken, beef, or shrimp) is not a bad idea either.

For ease, I like a purchased rotisserie chicken. Pull the meat off the bone and cut or pull into pieces.

It will make for a heartier meal.

RICE & RONI FROM SCRATCH – RICE AND PASTA TOGETHER WITH AN ADDITION OF TOMATO CHOWDER

THE COMBINATION IS A PERFECT MATCH.

BETTER THAN YOUR OLD SCHOOL SAN FRAN TREAT!

TOMATO CHICKEN MUSHROOM STEW

WHY THE HECK NOT?

This BONUS recipe is well worth your effort & time...
That's a joke, there is no effort or time – for the most part.

INGREDIENTS

Here's the list

- 2 C. Tomato Chowder – no need to warm or reduce.
- 1 lb. boneless skinless chicken thighs or breast. I prefer thighs. They always remain moist.
- Mushrooms – any you like. I prefer cremini for this dish - sliced ¼ in. thick.
- 1 large white or yellow onion – also sliced into ¼ in. pieces.
- I added sliced mushrooms & onions because my husband & I love them but put your own stamp on it.

STEPS

There are very few steps in this SHAKE-UP...

1

- Take your Chicken out of the fridge **30 minutes** prior to searing on medium heat in your Dutch oven.
- Season the chicken with salt, pepper & a sprinkling of cornstarch on both sides. The cornstarch will lend in thickening the stew.

Searing chicken thighs seasoned with salt, pepper & a light sprinkling of corn starch to help thicken the stew

2

- When the chicken is seared on both sides in 2 Tbsp. olive oil (**4 minutes** per side), remove from the pot & set aside while the sliced onions & mushrooms cook for **5 minutes**.

3

- At the same time, make your egg noodles.
- Cook to package directions. But drain them **2 minutes** prior.
- The stew is hot, so the noodles will continue to cook in the stew.

Raw chopped tomatoes added for freshness & brightness

4
- Bring back into the pot - chicken, your Tomato Chowder & some chicken stock if the stew is too thick, but that really shouldn't be necessary – the Chowder alone should do the job.

5
- Simmer the stew on medium low for about **30 minutes**.
- Due to the flavor in your Chowder, all that you are doing here is making sure the chicken is cooked through & that all the flavors have become one.

LAY A BED OF PASTA ON YOUR PLATES & SPOON OVER THE BEAUTIFUL STEW.

SOOTHING GOODNESS!

BEER CHEESE CHOWDER

INGREDIENTS

The usual BASE/DNA

- 1 lb. bacon

JUICY POTATO RECIPE

- 2 large Russet Potatoes
- 1 large or 2 medium Onions
- 1 tsp. Thyme – fresh or dried
- 1 tsp. Rosemary – fresh
- 2 Bay leaves
- 1 tsp. Salt
- ½ tsp. Pepper
- Splashes of chicken stock to keep the potatoes from sticking & burning – about ¼ C. max.

REMAINING INGREDIENTS

- 2 Celery stalks - chopped
- 2 big or 3 small carrots - chopped
- 2 Garlic Cloves - diced or grated
- 2 - 3 Qt. Chicken stock - all depends on how thin or thick you like Chowder.
- ½ Lager beer (6. oz)
- 1 C. Heavy Cream or Half & Half

STEPS

THIS CHOWDER IS PERFECT FOR A PARTY/CROWD – NOT THAT ALL CHOWDERS AREN'T.

It's almost like a Queso. It's cheesy, spicy (if you want it to be), & downright luxurious.

1

- Cook your bacon on medium low in a heavy bottomed pot until most of the fat has rendered.
- Remove the bacon to paper towels, chop into bite size pieces & set aside while you make **JUICY POTATOES**. The ingredients are on the side & also on **Pg. 8**.

2

- Sauté all the ingredients in 2 Tbsp. of butter (optional) & 1 Tbsp. of olive oil on medium low until the onions become translucent & the potatoes are crisp-tender – **10 minutes**.
- I'm telling you, after you make **JUICY POTATOES** once, the recipe will become a main stay in your life.

3

- Incorporate the chopped carrots & celery to the **JUICY POTATOES** as well as the reserved chopped bacon.

4

- Add the Stock & **MOST IMPORTANTLY YOUR BEER**, then simmer on low with the lid ajar, for **45 minutes**.
- After that, check for seasoning & adjust if needed.
- If the Chowder is too thin for your liking, take the lid off and simmer for another **15 – 20 minutes**.

****Keep in mind that the Chowder is going to thicken when you add cheese.***

5

- At that point, it's time to include your half & half or heavy cream – 1 C.
- Be sure that the heat is on low or better yet off the heat, so it doesn't curdle.

- Speaking of cheese, this is what I think is best in this Chowder:
- 1 C. Fontina – stirred into the Chowder once you are happy with the seasoning & texture.
- 1 C. Sharp Cheddar for the top of the bowls when serving.
- As mentioned, if you like spicy, add some Pepper Jack in place of half of the Fontina.

***You don't need to top with more cheese. You can just incorporate the cheddar into the pot with everything else.**

6

- The reason I top the bowls with extra cheese is because I love a good Brulé.
- To Brulé, merely put your hot bowls of Chowder on a sheet pan & broil them for about **3 minutes**, or until the cheese on top starts to turn golden brown.
- But, as I said, this Chowder is perfect even without that step.
- A bowl of good tortilla chips or a nice crusty bread is a match made in heaven for this Chowder.

I THINK YOU'LL BE MAKING THIS CHOWDER REGULARLY FOR GET TOGETHERS.

It's a definite GO-TO!

BEER CHEESE *Shake Ups*

1. Beer Cheese Poutine

2. Beer Cheese Chicken Alfredo

3. Chicken Lettuce Wrap

BEER CHEESE POUTINE

Prefer waffle fries?
With a great Chowder & cheese, it's rather tough to strike out with any fry you choose!

POUTINE topped with BEER CHOWDER CHEESE SAUCE.

It's kind of nuts good Watch out. These fries disappear!

Roasted fries topped with chopped mozzarella.

STEPS

A family favorite treat – especially on game day, movie or party night. To make it a very quick meal, buy frozen French fries.
I tried both frozen hand-cut fries & waffle/crinkle cut fries to see which works out best to stand up to the Chowder gravy/cheese sauce.

1 Bake the fries to package instructions while you are warming the sauce.

2 When warming the Beer Cheese Chowder (1 C.) in a saucepan on low heat, move onto the below suggestions:

3 Add more grated cheese (approximately 1 C.), to the warmed Chowder and stir to melt into a smooth cheese sauce. If your sauce separates, just add a tablespoon of cornstarch whisked together, with a ¼ C. stock or water in a small bowl or coffee cup & then and add to the sauce. The mixture will pull the sauce together.

4 Once the fries are done, lay them out on a large plate or just serve them on a sheet pan lined with foil if you have a crowd.

5 Top fries with the Chowder sauce & some cheese curds. Should you not be able to find cheese curds, add mozzarella cut up into ½ in. cubes instead.
If your family enjoys meat and potato type dinners, top the Poutine with any protein you would like – bacon, chicken, beef, etc. Typically, Poutine is topped with brown gravy and cheese curds, so this recipe is a different but delicious change up.

I'd be shocked if you & yours don't LOVE it!

IT MIGHT NOT BE THE HANDSOMEST OF DISHES, BUT IT'S TASTY & FUN TO EAT!

BRING ON THE COLD BEER OR COCKTAILS & LET THE GRAZING BEGIN!

SUGGESTIONS

An easy side salad with a fresh vinaigrette cut through the cheesy gravy Chowder sauce & fries.
Or, if it's an "I don't care about my diet until tomorrow day." Pair it with some baked frozen chicken tenders/nuggets.
I say just go for it and have all three

BEER CHEESE CHICKEN FETTUCCINI ALFREDO

ALFREDO SAUCE

- Addition of Chowder makes this Alfredo sauce much deeper in flavor than the typical butter, cream & cheese sauce – not that there is anything wrong with that!
- I like to spoon the Chowder (about 1 C.) in either a blender or a food processor to make it smooth & silky.

NOTE – You most certainly can skip this step if you are ok with pieces of veggies in the alfredo sauce.

- Once the Chowder is nice and homogenized, which will only take **a minute or less**, pour it into a large skillet and let it warm on low.

Here's where the creamy cheesiness comes into play...

To the smooth & silky Chowder, add the following...

- ½ C. Heavy Cream
- 4 TBSP. Butter
- ½ C. Grated Parmigiana Reggiano cheese

1

- Stir the Chowder & ingredients above together in your skillet. It will thicken nicely to coat the pasta.

STEPS

This Beer Cheese, Chicken Alfredo Shake-Up, is so quick & easy with the help of a store-bought rotisserie chicken, if you fancy

2

- Pull the chicken off the carcass into good sized bites and set aside.

If you want to make your own boneless skinless chicken breast, check out the suggestions below to ensure it ends up perfect.

Here's the path to perfectly seasoned & moist chicken every time

3

- Season the chicken (after patting dry with paper towels,) with salt & pepper, when you remove it from the fridge. The seasoning creates a dry brine so when you sear it in the pan, it creates a nice brown crust. Again, always make sure the chicken is at room temperature before searing it in the pan.

Golden brown chicken is GOOD!

4

- After **20 or so minutes** have passed, heat your skillet to medium.
- Place the chicken breasts into an oiled skillet (1 - 2 TBSP. of olive oil).
- It takes about **4 minutes** per side to cook a good-sized chicken breast. It seems today that they are quite large.

5

- After you take the chicken out of your pan, let it rest for a good **5 – 10 minutes** before slicing it. That way you don't lose the juices & the chicken ends up beautifully moist.

6 Once the chicken has rested, slice it into whatever size pieces you want.
I like to think of it this way - If you can fit it on your fork with a roll of pasta around it, you're good!

7 What remains - make the fettuccini - always **2 minutes** less than the package directions (as usual) and marry everything together in the skillet once the pasta is done.

8 Stir it all together - pasta, chicken & Chowder sauce.
Feel free to top with more grated Parmigiana Reggiano. Tell me what's wrong with that?
This is an Alfredo you haven't had before. It certainly did not come out of a jar. The flavor has so much depth due to the zipped/blended Chowder.

GRAB YOUR FORK & SPOON (IF YOU ROLL THAT WAY WITH PASTA) &

ENJOY THE INDULGENCE!

CHICKEN LETTUCE WRAP

Chowder poured onto the chicken wrap. YUM!

Chicken Lettuce Crema & Pico

STEPS

1

- As with most ***SHAKE-UPs***, warm & reduce your Chowder (1 C.) in a saucepan over low heat while you sear the chicken – **or not.**

***By all means, sear your own chicken breasts or thighs, but a rotisserie chicken from the store is ideal here.**

- Due to the flavorful chowder, you can do this with your eyes closed. Almost

Time to make your way to the table…

2

- Pile your pulled or chopped chicken (whichever you choose), onto some iceberg lettuce.
- I prefer iceberg for this it has muscle if you know what I mean. it will stand up to the chicken & chowder & stay crunchy.

3

- Spoon over your warm chowder.

4

- **DRIZZLE** on SOME crema & Pico if that's how you groove.

HOPE YOUR FAMILY IS READY - BECAUSE DINNER IS SERVED!

FRENCH ONION SOUP CHOWDER

THIS CHOWDER IS SO SIMPLE & TASTY.

If you enjoy French onion soup, this recipe & the Shake-Ups, are right up your alley. It's downright mouthwatering. Let's get onto it.

STEPS

1
- **Preheat your oven to 425**.
- Make the **Base/DNA (pg. 5)** in your Dutch oven or heavy bottomed pot and remove it to a bowl or dish and set aside.

2
- Add a couple tbsp. of butter & a couple tbsp. of olive oil to the same pot you made the base.

3

To the butter & olive oil add:
- 5 large or 6 small yellow onions – you can also use white. Slice your yellow or white onions into approximately ¼ in. Slices. It's amazing how much they will cook down.
- 2 bay leaves
- 1 tbsp. Of fresh or dried thyme,1 tbsp. Coarse salt, and ½ tbsp. Black pepper

****NOTE: keep the lid on the pot – ajar - while you are cooking the onions.***

- When you first put them in the pot, on medium – low, it looks like a mountain of onions, but in **30 minutes** or so, they will render down to a quarter of the original amount. It takes time for the onions to caramelize & become very soft – **30 – 40 minutes** – as previously mentioned

4
- While you are cooking the onions down, add a splash of water or stock when needed, if they start looking too dry & begin to stick to the bottom of your pan.

Once the onions are completely soft add:
- 4 grated or finely chopped garlic cloves
- ¼ C. Soy, tamari or liquid amino
- 2 Tbsp. Worcestershire sauce
- ¼ C. sherry or brandy. You can also use bourbon or a good quality whisky if that's what you have.

5
- Put the chowder base back into the pot with the onions.

6
- The final addition is stock: 2 - 3 qt. Of chicken or beef stock - whatever you prefer. You can always add more if you need it.

7 Let the chowder cook on low for **30 minutes** while you make croutons & slice some gruyere cheese. You can also use cheddar.

Feel free to purchase croutons from the store, or easily make your own out of stale bread. This is how you do it...

8
- Cut your bread - into ½ in. square pieces & put them into a large bowl. Any bread is fine, but I like a chewy sourdough for this.
- Sprinkle the bread with a couple tbsp. of olive oil & pinch of salt & black pepper.
- The addition of a little granulated garlic & or granulated onion is your call. I like a flavorful crouton for this dish.

9 Mix the cubed bread together in the large bowl & pour them onto a foil lined baking sheet. Depending on the stale-ness of your bread, it should take around **8 - 10 minutes** for a supple crouton & **12 minutes (on 425)** for a crispier finish - again, your call.

10
- As for cheese, I prefer Gruyere, but you can also use a Sharp Cheddar or even Muenster. To round the corner quicker, have the cheese section of your grocery store slice it for you.
- Thin slices work well so you can layer as much as you want on top of the chowder. I like a good amount of cheese on this chowder – say ¼ lb. per bowl.

11
- After **30 minutes** or so, ladle your chowder into oven proof bowls & top with croutons & cheese.
- Place the bowls on a sheet pan & broil on low until the cheese starts to golden.

SWEET ONIONS, SAVORY DEEP JUS, GARLICKY CROUTONS & THAT STRINGY CHEESE.

HERE COMES ONE LOVELY CHEESE COMA!

FRENCH ONION *Shake Ups*

1. *Linguini with Shrimp & Scallops*
2. *Croque Monsieur/Madame*
3. *Vegetable Rice Noodle Bowl*
4. *Bonus – Chicken Marsala*

Bon Appetit

LINGUINI WITH SHRIMP & SCALLOPS

A decadent dish for a special occasion or just causes.

HIGHLIGHTS

Here's the Roadmap.

- You can use just shrimp if you want for this recipe, but a few seared scallops take this dish over the top.

AS A NOTE - most shellfish are frozen on ice the second it's thrown into the fishing boat, so don't spend the extra dollars on fresh, (it's been frozen too - most likely). Lay the fish onto paper towels to defrost for about 20 minutes.

STEPS

1
- After the fish is defrosted, salt & pepper both sides.
- It won't be long until the entire dish comes together, so the seasoned fish can sit for a few minutes.

2
- Begin the typical *Shake-Up* routine by warming
- 1 ½ C. of Chowder in a small saucepan & let it sit/rest with a lid on until the pasta & fish is finished.

3
- Pasta - Using a large pot – 6 Qt. or larger, fill it ¾ with cold water and bring to a boil on high heat.
- When the water comes to a rapid boil, add a couple Tbsp. of salt, or more. If it doesn't taste like the sea, add more salt. Remember, we are making a seafood dish.
- As always, boil your pasta **2 minutes** less than the package directions so it remains al dente.

Let's Go Finishing

If you're not accustomed to making shellfish, this dish will boost your confidence – you'll be making it regularly.

4
- To a large sauté pan on medium high heat, add a Tbsp. of olive oil & the same amount of butter.
- When the oil & butter starts to ripple, it's time to start searing the fish. Don't let the butter brown or it will get bitter. You're only looking for a little froth (small golden bubbles), in the oil & butter.

5
- Put the shrimp on one side of the pan & on the other side, put the scallops – this way you don't need to use two pans & create more dishes.
- As for cooking time on the shrimp & scallops, here it is:
- **1 ½ minutes** per side for both the shrimp & scallops – tough, right?
- I know it sounds quite quick, but when all is stirred together, everything will be **PERFECT!**

6

- Drain the pasta once your timer goes off – **2 minutes** short of the package directions. I know I repeat myself, but it's worth repeating so that you end up with an amazing dish!
- Keep a cup of the starchy water on the side, in case you need to smooth out the sauce in the end.

7

- Now put the pasta right back into the pot & pour in your warmed Chowder to marry them together.
- Stir it all together with a couple dashes of starchy pasty water – only if it's too tight.
- Plate the Chowder pasta and top with your sautéed shrimp & scallops.

HOW THE HECK IS THIS A SHAKE-UP OF FRENCH ONION SOUP CHOWDER?

Crazy!

CROQUE MONSIEUR/MADAME

Think upside-down French onion soup

Crouton is on the bottom, rendered French Onion Chowder, on top, cheese & beautiful sunny side egg (if you're going Madame), tops it all off!

STEPS

Here's the details for another simple, delicious comforting dish, so you can relax after a long hard day.

Toasted bread slathered with Chowder & sliced cheese. back in the oven to Get your melt on!

1 Toast bread in the toaster or in your oven until it's golden brown & crispy – a nice Italian bread or a good baguette works well since they are crustier.

2 Warm 1 ½ C. Chowder in a saucepan on medium low until it comes to a simmer & cooks down to thicken. You'll know it's ready when the bubbles get bigger in size. It will probably take about **10 minutes**.

3 Top the toast with Chowder & some grated or sliced Swiss cheese and broil it until the cheese browns. Depending on your oven, it should take about **3 minutes**.

4 Now, if you are like me, an egg on top (Croque Madame), makes any dish better. With that said, top the finished dish with a sunny side egg or not. Without the egg you have a Croque Masseur.

EGG INSTRUCTIONS

The simplest & tastiest way to make sunny side up eggs is to start with an oven proof non-stick skillet lined with a TBSP. of butter or olive oil OR, better yet, one TBSP. of butter and one TBSP. of olive oil combined. The butter and olive oil together on low heat communicate well with each other – the flavor is amazing. Sunny side up eggs are called that for an obvious reason.

The yolk resembles the beautiful rising sun.

5

- When the whites of the eggs start to firm & the yolk is still very yellow, put the pan under the broiler for **2 minutes**.
- Check on the yolks halfway through to be sure they are staying bright yellow & not over cooking – we're not looking for hard egg yolks. If you don't have a broiler, place the eggs in a 450 oven instead. It works just as well.
- We want a nice runny egg yolk to act as a luxurious sauce over the open-faced sandwich. After **3 minutes** they should look like a ladies BONNETT – Very yellow in the middle and opaque white on the outside.

A wink at Croque Monsieur, or even better, in my eyes, Croque Madame (topped with an egg) – you must make this!

PLACE THE EGGS ONTO THE OPEN-FACED CHEESE SANDWICH. YOU WON'T BELIEVE HOW SIMPLE AND DECADENT THIS MIDWEEK DINNER TURNS OUT.

Whether you top this dish with eggs OR NOT, it's going to be a diverse and enjoyable dinner!

VEGETABLE RICE NOODLE BOWL

If you regularly order out for Asian food, this will save you – in time and money.
Not to mention, you know all the ingredients.
Can't beat that.

SLURP IT UP

WHO WOULD THINK OF IT? A NOODLE BOWL MADE FROM FRENCH ONION SOUP CHOWDER!

HIGHLIGHTS

1 • If using mushrooms, cut into ½-inch slices (cremini, shitake, or button if you would like), then sauté them in a small amount of olive oil in your pot don't salt them until they start to brown, otherwise they will release their water and not brown properly.

2 • Once the mushrooms are nicely seared, which will take about **5 minutes**, season with salt, pepper & remove them to a plate.

3 • Add & sauté whatever other vegetables you would like to use - broccoli, cauliflower, snap peas, canned water chestnuts, to the same pot you used to sear the mushrooms with another drizzle of oil.

Coming up - The remaining recipe details.

STEPS

1
- Chop vegetables into approximately 1-inch pieces - whichever vegetables you like in a stir-fry, i.e., broccoli, mushrooms, cauliflower, snap peas, canned water chestnuts.
- Any vegetables you and your family enjoy will do. You need about 2 C. vegetables. Remember, the veggies from the Chowder will be included as well.

2 Speaking of Chowder, warm about a 1 C. in a saucepan on low heat.

3

- As the Chowder is warming, making the rice noodles isn't a bad idea. It's a very complicated process – waiting around for a few minutes doing absolutely nothing.

***You can use any type of Asian noodles you want, but for this dish, I like glass/cellophane noodles.**

- The flat (linguini looking) rice noodles are great here as well. You should easily be able to find these types of noodles in the international isle of your grocery store.
- Soak the cellophane or rice noodles in lukewarm water in a large bowl for about **25 minutes**.

The noodles will still be quite al dente, but they will continue to cook for a couple minutes in the stir-fry sauce – I told you it was complex.

SAUTÉED VEGETABLES THAT WILL BE AN ADDITION TO WARMED CHOWDER & RICE NOODLES

BONUS –CHICKEN MARSALA

French Onion Chowder with the addition of chicken & mushrooms.

STEPS

A beautiful SHAKE-UP for any day of the week.

1
- Warm the Chowder (1. C) in a small saucepan on low – just until it's warm. You can strain the Chowder with a slotted spoon, but it isn't necessary in this recipe. **The Chowder is your sauce.** I strained the Chowder simply to make it a little prettier to photograph.
- I added a splash (2 Tbsp.) of Marsala wine – it is Marsala after all, but that's your call. The Chowder alone is flavorful enough to make a delicious dish.

2
- 1 Boneless skinless chicken breast per person is plenty for this **SHAKE-UP**.
- Season with salt & pepper. I like granulated onion & granulated garlic on chicken as well. When you can boost the flavor of a dish, why not?

****With that said, keep in mind that your Chowder is seasoned, so don't go overboard.***

3
- Sear the chicken in a non-stick skillet drizzled with 1 Tbsp. olive oil – **6 minutes** per side, on medium heat.

4
- Remove the chicken & set aside to rest for **5 minutes** before slicing, so the juices remain in the chicken & don't run out all over your plate.

5
- Slice your mushrooms (button or cremini) OR purchase them that way (sliced) from the grocery.

6
- Sear the mushrooms with 1 Tbsp. Olive Oil, on medium high in the same pan you seared the chicken. No need at all for seasoning here. There will be some seasoning left in the pan from the chicken. Once you put the mushrooms in the pan, let them lie for a few minutes until moving them around. Searing brings taste & texture.

7
- Stir together the mushrooms & warmed Chowder.

8
- Slice the chicken & pour over your Chowder sauce.
- As you can see, I chose to sear green beans seasoned with olive oil, salt & pepper. Feel free to use any side your family enjoys. Fresh green beans, mashed potatoes, simple side salad, snap peas, garlic bread – just some ideas that would be delicious alongside this Chicken Marsala dish.

Your Marsala Shake-Up has arrived – ENJOY!

MEATLOAF CHOWDER

INGREDIENTS

- 2 lb. ground meat - I use ground turkey, but you can use beef or a combination of both.
- 1 sautéed carrot,
- 2 stalks of celery,
- 1 small onion (all diced)
- This Chowder starts by making the meatloaf. You'll need Pressed Roasted Meatloaf

STEPS

1

- Once the veg are tender-crisp, put in a bowl to cool for 5 minutes.

Then add in your meat.

- 1 egg to bind everything together
- 1 Tbsp. Salt & ½ Tbsp. Pepper – remember this is 2 lbs. of meat.

2

- Mix it all together, then press out on a foil lined sheet pan (brushed with olive oil) – as pictured above.

3

- **Bake at 375 for 25 minutes**. Once done, let it rest until it cools a bit, then cut it into bite size pieces. While the meatloaf is baking, pull the base together & add it to your pot.

4

- As always, start with **JUICY POTATOES (Pg. 8)**, then move onto the rest of the **base (Pg. 5)**.

5

- Cook the base for about **10 minutes** or until the veggies begin to soften - don't cook the veggies through, Once the Chowder is all put together, it is going to cook for **an hour** & you don't want the veggies to disappear.

Here is where it gets really difficult. WINK WINK

6
Add the following:
- 3 - 4 QTs. of Chicken Stock – 3 if you like a heartier Chowder, 4 if you prefer it soupier.
- 2 28 oz. cans of good tomatoes. As you add them to the pot, crush them with your hands to break them up a bit. Your cubed meatloaf pieces.
- 2 TBSP. salt
- 1 TBSP. pepper

7
- Put a lid on your pot, keeping it ajar so some steam can escape.
- Cook on medium- low for **45 minutes**, stirring every **20 minutes**.

8
- After that, give it a taste for seasoning & texture. If it's too thin for your taste, cook it down another **15 - 30 minutes** with the lid off.

9
- Once you're happy with the taste & texture, add 1 C. heavy cream or half & half – stir it all together.

THATS ALL SHE WROTE!

MEATLOAF *Shake Ups*

1. *Meatloaf Stuffed Peppers*
2. *Meatloaf Chowder Cheesy Dip*
3. *Meatloaf Sandwiches*

MEATLOAF STUFFED PEPPERS

STEPS

1
- Begin these amazing Stuffed Peppers by warming some of your Chowder in a medium saucepan – about 2 C. for 4 – 6 servings - from 4 whole Bell Peppers.
- You won't believe how hearty these are. This is an (eyes are bigger than your stomach), situation.

2
- As for the long grain rice (basmati or jasmine), just follow the package directions.
- With that said, please use stock (chicken or vegetable), instead of water, or better yet, ½ portion stock & ½ portion whole milk or half & half. You won't believe the difference in flavor.

- After the rice is done, fluff it with a fork or spoon & set it aside off the heat, until your peppers are ready to be stuffed.

Here's the stuffing ingredients

3
- Warmed chowder – broken up a bit with a fork.
- ½ lb. Ground Turkey
- ½ C. Grated Parmesan Cheese
- 1 tsp. Granulated Onion & Garlic
- 1 tsp. Oregano
- ½ tsp. Thyme – fresh is best but dried still creates a lovely flavor.
- ¼ tsp. Chili Flake – personally, I would use ½ tsp., but you spice it up as much as you want.

Strain the meat out of the Chowder for your stuffing with a slotted spoon. The Chowder sauce will be used for topping the peppers.

4
- Mix the rice together along with the rest of the stuffing ingredients in a large bowl and let sit for a couple minutes. It's better if the stuffing is room temperature before going into the oven.

Long grain rice - the binder that holds stuffed peppers together.

5
- Time to remove the ribs and seeds from the peppers.

NOTE: Removing the ribs and seeds is nothing.

- Slice off the top of the pepper – the stem end (green end).
- Take a kitchen tablespoon & remove the ribs & seeds so that you have enough room for the meatloaf filling. Using a tablespoon helps a ton so that you don't break the pepper! A broken pepper does not make for a great stuffed pepper.

6
- Spoon the filling into the peppers & pat it down. Make sure the filling is pressed into the pepper, without going as far as tearing it.

7
- All that's left is putting the stuffed peppers in your pot & top with Chowder sauce & some more marinara – homemade or store bought until you have 3 C. total – or more if you like it extra saucy.
- They will need about **40 minutes** on medium low heat to cook through (depending on the size of peppers you're using).
- I suggest putting a lid or a piece of foil on top of the pot, while the stuffed peppers are cooking, so that the sauce creates minimal mess on your stove.

The beauty of this dish is you virtually can't over cook it due to the combination of meat, rice, cheese, sauce & the moisture from the bell pepper.

Stuffed peppers with mashed meatloaf Chowder, ground turkey & rice

THESE WILL RING YOUR BELL!

THEY ARE NOTHING OTHER THAN LUXURIOUS!

MEATLOAF CHOWDER CHEESY DIP

ONE LOOK AT THIS CHEESY DIP & YOU MUST MAKE THIS FOR YOU & YOURS.

It's ooey gooey & unbelievably delicious!
Get out your warm flour tortillas, tortilla chips, or even some veggies.
It's a good thing!

STEPS

1

- As usual, warm some of your Chowder in a saucepan, 2 ½ C. should work well for 4 – 6 servings.
- **Preheat your oven to 350**.
- Onto the best part, the **CHEESE SAUCE!** There are many cheeses that would be great for this dish, but I'll tell you how I made the version you see here.

2

- Start by making a simple Bechamel in a saucepan,
- Add 3 TBSP. butter & 3 TBSP. flour.
- Warm until the butter has melted & it resembles wet sand.

3

- At this point whisk in 3 C. milk until it all comes together & there aren't any lumps.
- Simmer the roux on medium low until it thickens. It will coat the back of a spoon when it's done.
- Turn the heat down on low to keep warm.

Best part is next – CHEESE!

4

I like the following grated cheese for this dish:

- Gruyere
- Sharp Cheddar
- Fontina

- Grate about ½ C. of each cheese and stir it into the roux. If the cheese sauce is too loose, add a little more.

NOTE – Remember that you are going to be adding Chowder to the cheese sauce which will thin it some.

All said, the Chowder is somewhat thick on its own right, so tread lightly with adding too much cheese.
As if there is such a thing, right?!?

5

- In your saucepan of Chowder, add the thickened cheesy roux & stir together to get a feel for thickness/texture.
- If it's a **little thick**, add a little stock
- If it's **on the thin side**, add some more of your meatloaf Chowder – mostly the tender pieces of meat.

6

- Using olive oil, butter or both, grease an oven-safe casserole dish.
- Pour it all in there & top the casserole with a nice layer of grated cheese.
- It will brown nicely in the oven – ½ C. cheese will do.

Should you want to stretch this out into a larger dish, simply put your Meatloaf Dip in a soft corn tortilla, top with some Pico, Sour Cream & shredded lettuce & it's a WRAP!

IN LESS THAN 20 MINUTES, YOU HAVE AN AMAZING DECADENT DISH THAT CAN BE DINNER OR A FABULOUS SNACK TO HAVE WITH COMPANY.

TELL ME YOUR GUESTS WOULDN'T DEVOURER THIS ON GAME DAY!

MEATLOAF SANDWICHES

TO END ALL, MEATLOAF SANDWICHES!

A sandwich roll can be controversial.
Some like a soft roll & some prefer a tougher roll.
In this instance, I like a sturdy roll due to the meaty Chowder, but they all will work.

STEPS

1 Feel free to use a roll straight from the store or bakery if you want, but with this sandwich being so hearty, toasting it in the oven **at 375 for 5 minutes**, holds it together nicely.

2 Olive oil & Mayo on a cheesy, tomatoey meatloaf sandwich is my choice, but there is absolutely nothing wrong with mustard either.

3 For the cheese, the easiest is a nice sliced cheddar, but you can use a good All American as well.

4 Pile your **COLD** or **ROOM TEMP** Meatloaf squares from the Chowder on top of the cheese.

Sandwich roll layered with slices of cheddar cheese and Warmed meatloaf Chowder on cheese. on one side & pickles on the other - dill or bread & butter.

Whatever tickles your pickle!

- Layer your Pickles on the other side of the bread.

I love dill & garlic. Bread & butter pickles are not a bad choice either, if that's how you roll – no pun intended.

I think it's now obvious that this recipe is about to hit the goal line…

- Squeeze it all together & chomp down.

5
- I chose to make a side arugula salad dressed with olive oil, balsamic vinegar, Dijon mustard, salt, pepper & a tiny drizzle of honey or agave.
- Mix the dressing together in a large bowl – taste for seasoning - top with the arugula. Wait to toss the salad together until you are ready to plate. That way, your greens will not wilt & get soggy.

THIS SHAKE-UP SHOULD BE ON YOUR REGULAR FAMILY MENU

COCONUT CURRY CHOWDER

HARISSA
Hot Chili Pepper Paste with added spices & herbs. You can find this in the international isle of your grocery store.
A little goes a long way!
Use the best quality **tomato paste** your grocery store has. If you're not sure of the best brands, ask the store employees. They will direct you. This will also be in the international isle or next to the Italian canned tomatoes. In most stores they will most likely be in the same isle.
DOUBLE CONCENTRATED
TOMATO PASTE
100% Italiano

THIS CHOWDER IS SWEET, SPICY, CREAMY & COMFORTING.

STEPS

1
- Start by rendering down your bacon– preferably in a ceramic lined cast iron pot.
- Remove your bacon to the side & chop it into bite size pieces.

2
- Season the chicken on both sides with salt, pepper, cumin, coriander & some cayenne – if you are spicy like me. 2 lb. of chicken is right on for this recipe.

3 ♘ Sear your chicken in the same pot on medium heat.

That's one of the beauties of my chowders, they are made in one pot.
Most of the time, I prefer boneless skinless thighs, but in this instance, I had boneless skinless chicken breast on hand so that is what I used.

♘ If you decide on chicken thighs, they will take approximately **8 minutes** per side.

♘ If you go with chicken breasts, they will take no longer than **5 minutes** per side.

Be sure your chicken is room temp before you begin searing it in your pot.

4 ♘ Once the chicken is well seared on both sides, take it out of the pot & put aside with the rendered bacon to rest for **a couple minutes**.

5 ♘ After the chicken has rested, chop it into bite size pieces so that it will fit onto your spoon along with everything else in the Chowder.

♘ When you cut up the chicken, if it's undercooked, no worries. It will definitely finish cooking through in the pot with everything else.

As with any poultry, ALWAYS wash your hands after handling & prior to touching anything else.
Cross contamination is beyond a bummer & can make you very ill.

Now, go figure – JUICY POTATOES:

- 2 large Russet Potatoes
- 1 Large or 2 medium Onions
- 1 tsp. Thyme – fresh or dried
- 1 tsp. Rosemary – fresh
- 2 Bay leaves
- 1 tsp. Salt ½ tsp. Pepper
- Splashes of chicken stock to keep the potatoes from sticking & burning

Further down the recipe, add...

- 2 Celery stalks – chopped
- 2 big or 3 small carrots – chopped
- 2 Garlic Cloves
- 2 – 3 Qt. Chicken stock – all depends on how thin or thick you like Chowder.

Directions are next.

6 ♘ After you have seared the meat & made **JUICY POTATOES**, it is now time to include the carrots, celery & chopped garlic with everything else in the pot.

♘ Since the carrots & celery are such dense vegetables, adding them closer to the end is perfect. It helps to keep a good amount of their structure & integrity. This way you won't have whimp limp vegetables, but a chowder that's deep, not only in flavor, but also texture.

7 ♘ Speaking of flavor, it's time to add 1 - 2 Tbsp. of Harissa.

♘ Stir it in so the flavor will bloom into the base.

♘ Should you not be a fan of spicy food, stick with 1 Tbsp.

If you're like me & my husband & really love spicy food, put in 2 Tbsp.

8 ♘ Add 2 Tbsp. of tomato paste, 1 Tbsp. of light brown sugar, 1 in. grated ginger, 2 Tbsp. curry powder & stir until incorporated.

9

- Place your chopped bacon & chicken back into the pot.

10

- Add your stock (2 – 3 Qtrs.).

OPTIONAL: I chose to add 1 oz. cooked rice noodles per bowl when serving the finished Chowder.

- Simple cook to package directions & add as much as you want to each bowl of Chowder when serving if you wish. Again, certainly, **NOT** necessary.
- Now it's time to take the Chowder over the top...

11

- Put in a can of coconut milk. Typically, the cans come in 13.5 or 14 oz. That's the perfect amount to pull the flavors in this Chowder together.
- It will round out the base to taste like your favorite take away curry bowl.

TIPS

- The coconut milk takes over for the heavy cream or half & half that's in Chowders. There is no need for cream here.
- Once everything cooks together on medium low for **45 minutes**, the Chowder is ready to be devoured!

GRAND SHAKE-UPS TO FOLLOW!

COCONUT CURRY *Shake Ups*

1. *Chicken Meatballs with Rice Noodles*
2. *Coconut Curry Fried Rice*
3. *Coconut Curry Chicken Wings*

CHICKEN MEATBALLS WITH RICE NOODLES

I love making meatballs of all kind.
Whether that be beef, pork, chicken, turkey or any combination of meats you prefer. They're all scrumptious!

The beauty of meatballs is the versatility. Most think of beef & pork when it comes to meatballs, but once you experiment with chicken & turkey, it will change your thoughts on what a meatball is, or should I say – can be.

For this Curry Shake-Up recipe, I really love a delicate chicken meatball.

If you've never enjoyed a chicken meatball, you're in for a serious treat!

INGREDIENTS

- ½ C. Panko breadcrumbs
- ¼ C. Whole milk or Half & Half
- 1 tsp. Granulated Garlic
- 1 tsp. Granulated Onion – or onion powder
- 1 tsp. Dried Oregano
- ½ tsp. Chili Flakes – Pepperoncini
- 1 ½ tsp. Salt
- ¾ tsp. Black Pepper
- ½ C. Grated Parmesan Cheese

STEPS

Speaking of that, let's make some chicken meatballs, shall we...

1
- To 1 lb. of ground white meat chicken, in a large mixing bowl, add all the ingredients.

2
- Mix all the above ingredients together. It's best to use your hands, but you can use a large spoon if you want.
- When it comes to mixing ground meat, the **LAST** thing you want to do is over mix. Your meatballs will turn out tough instead of nice and tender – nice & tender is better than tough!

3
- Line a baking sheet with foil and brush with a light coating of olive oil.

4
- Roll the meatballs into about 1 in. pieces and place them on the oiled sheet pan.
- You can also use a small ice cream scoop to ensure that all the meatballs are the same size and cook evenly.

5
- Place them in a **preheated 375 oven for 15 – 20 minutes**. They will continue to cook in the curry base.

Now onto the Curry Chowder portion of the dish...

6
- Scoop out 2 C. Chowder base.
- Leave behind the chicken for Shake-Ups. There will be plenty of chicken due to the meatballs.

7
- Warm your chowder on low for **10 minutes** or so, until it's warmed through & rendered some.

8
- Add the baked chicken meatballs to the curry.

Oven baked Meatballs in Coconut Curry Chowder

9
- One last ingredient to this amazing dish is to just add rice noodles 6 oz. for 4 to 6 Servings.
- There should be enough liquid to cook the noodles, but if not, add a little chicken stock or water.
- Making rice noodles is not like making semolina pasta. It only takes **2 – 3 minutes** in a small amount of liquid for them to cook to al dente.
- You can see in the photo aside that there isn't much liquid in the pot when adding the rice noodles – that's what you want.

We aren't making soup here; this is a Meatball Noodle Curry dish.

Addition of rice or cellophane noodles to the curry.

YOU WON'T BELIEVE THAT THIS IS A SHAKE-UP OF A CHOWDER.

YOUR ENTIRE HOUSE WILL SMELL INTOXICATING!

CHICKEN FRIED RICE

FRIED RICE AT HOME IS FUN!

It's quick & the amazing aromas that surround your home are intoxicating

STEPS

1 ⍉ Warm 2 C. of your Chowder on low with 1 C. Chicken/Veg Stock. It's the liquid to make your fluffy rice.

2 ⍉ Measure 1 ½ C. long grain rice (Jasmine or Basmati) & add it to the warmed Chowder & Stock.
⍉ Cook **2 minutes** short of package directions.
⍉ VEG – Whatever tickles your fancy – Broccoli, Cauliflower, Carrots, Onions, Snap Peas, etc.

I went with simple broccoli & mushrooms because they were in the fridge.

3 ⍉ Chop the veg into small pieces – to co-mingle with your rice.

4 ⍉ In a sauté pan, sprinkled with 2 Tbsp. Olive Oil, sear the veg over high heat for **2 minutes**.
⍉ Whatever veg you use; high heat & quick searing is key to texture in the finished Shake-Up.

5 ⍉ Once the rice is done, mix it together in your sauté pan with the veg.

6 ⍉ On HIGH heat, stir-fry it all together for **1 – 2 minutes**.

THATS IT. SMILE & ENJOY YOUR HOMECOOKED TAKEAWAY!

COCONUT CURRY CHICKEN WINGS

YOUR FRIENDS & FAMILY WILL THINK THIS WING & RICE DISH WAS DROPPED AT YOUR DOOR. | *JOKE'S ON THEM!*

Time to warm up - and by warm up, I mean your oven for these wings.
Preheat your oven to 450. I know, I'm cheeky at best!

STEPS

1
- Take the wings out of the refrigerator – salt & pepper both sides and let them come to room temp. It takes about **20 - 30 minutes**.

2
- Separately, in a small sauté pan on low, warm 1.C Coconut Curry Chowder on low for it to cook down & thicken a bit – you want it to nicely coat the wings.
- While the wings are sitting & the Chowder is warming, it's a great time to make the rice. This rice can be served warm or room temp – both ways are wonderful – which is why you can make it ahead of baking the wings.

3
- Make the long grain rice (Jasmine or Basmati), according to the package directions – minus **1 – 2 minutes** so that it doesn't get soggy.
- When making 4 – 6 servings, I go with 1 C. rice. It will result in plenty for this wing & rice dish combo.

****Note - it's SOO much tastier to make the rice in chicken stock instead of water. I've even eaten the leftover rice straight out of the fridge in the morning – no shame!***

4
- As the rice is cooking, chop up what makes this **GREEN RICE…**
- 1 C. finely chopped fresh baby spinach
- ¼ C. chopped scallions
- If you like cilantro, a ¼ C. would brighten the rice as well.

Roasted wings prior to getting slathered with Chowder Sauce

AFTER TAKING A BATH IN REDUCED CHOWDER

5
- Put the chopped greens into a bowl – a large enough bowl so that you can mix the rice & greens together without having to dirty anything else.
- Set aside until the rice is done.

Let's get back to the WINGS

6
- A sheet pan lined with foil topped with a lightly oiled wire rack is the best way to make baked wings. **The wire rack is NOT a must**. That way, the heat is distributed all around the wings. The result is delicious crispy baked wings.

7
- If you are making whole wings, i.e., the drumette, flat wingette & tip all still together, put them in the oven to roast for **45 minutes**.
- On the other hand, if your wings are broken into drumettes & wingettes, they will only take **35 minutes** to roast.

8
- The rice should be done by now, so stir it together with the greens.
- Your beautiful side dish of green rice will be waiting happily for the main dish – **COCONUT CURRY WINGS!**

9
- Once the wings come out of the oven, toss them with the rendered Chowder in a large bowl until they are all perfectly coated.

What fun - Get your WING on!

QUESO CHOWDER

This isn't the lightest of Chowders, but for an occasion, or just for the fun of it...
Give it a shot.
Here is how this Chowder goes down

STEPS

1

- Make the base/DNA (Pg. 5).

2

- Add 2 C. grated cheese tossed with 1 Tbsp. of cornstarch. The cornstarch will keep the cheese from separating.
- Gruyere, Cheddar, Monetary Jack/Pepper Jack or any other of your favorite melting cheese works.
- My main suggestion when it comes to cheese - if you don't feel secure in this area, the cheese department at your grocery, will be happy to help you.

3

- I know this sounds ridiculous, but all you have to do for this Chowder is combine the base/DNA with your cheese/cornstarch & 3 QTS. of chicken stock.

The final piece of the puzzle for this recipe is the topping

4

- Stir everything together over low heat & it should be ready in **10 minutes** or less.
- I added some Pico at the end for brightness & spice. A nicely toasted piece of bread is a great accompaniment, or just go in there with your spoon.

SUCH A COMFORTING CHOWDER

PUT ON YOUR PJS OR SWEATS & HUNKER DOWN!

QUESO CHOWDER *Shake Ups*

1. Queso Chicken Broccoli Bake
2. Chicken Fingers & Fries with Queso Chowder Dip
3. Chicken Chopped Salad with Quesadilla Croutons

QUESO CHICKEN BROCCOLI BAKE

Once the bake is bubbling around the edges and the topping is golden brown,

DINNER IS ON THE TABLE – ALMOST…

It is imperative to ALWAYS let any baked dish rest for about 10 minutes before serving, so it sets up and doesn't run all over your plate & scorch your mouth!

STEPS

1

- **Preheat your oven to 375** & lightly oil or butter your casserole dish (9x9 works), so the bake doesn't stick.

2

- Reduce 1 ½ C. Chowder (for 4 – 6 Servings), in a medium saucepan on low heat.
- It will take approximately **10 minutes**. Be sure to stir the Chowder every few minutes so it doesn't stick to the bottom of the pan.
- You'll know the Chowder is reduced enough when you run your finger down the middle of the back of your wooden spoon (plastic works fine as well), and the Chowder leaves a clear path that stays separated.

Time to mix in the veggies:

3

- Broccoli – cut into bite sized pieces. A small head of broccoli should be enough.
- Frozen Peas – ½ to 1/3 C. – You can use more if you love peas or less if they aren't your favorite, but I think they have a place in this dish.
- **Optional** – A few diced Scallions – since there is already onions in the Chowder, it's not important, but it adds a freshness along with broccoli and peas.
- **Optional** – A few dashes of hot sauce can heighten the flavor as well. That's completely up to you.

The final piece of the puzzle for this recipe is the topping

4

- Mix together in a bowl,1/3 C. Panko breadcrumbs with ¼ C. grated Parmigiano Reggiano cheese and a drizzle of olive oil – about 1 Tbsp – maybe a tiny bit more, depending on how much topping you want on your bake.

5

- Top the casserole dish of Chowder & veggie filling with the Panko Parmigiano mixture and put in the preheated oven.
- Bake for **25 minutes** covered with foil and another **10 minutes** uncovered.

Grab your spoon & have at it. don't burn your mouth!

CHICKEN FINGERS & FRIES WITH QUESO CHOWDER DIP

Let's start with the chicken....

STEPS

1

- **Preheat your oven to 400**.
- Take your chicken breast out of the refrigerator at least **15 minutes** prior to baking time. It's best that the chicken, or any protein for that matter, be room temp prior to cooking.
- For 4 -6 servings, you'll need 6 breasts or about 2 lb.

2

- While the chicken is coming to room temp, heat ½ C. of the Chowder in a saucepan on low to reduce. It should take the same amount of time to reduce as it does the chicken to come to room temp & ready to coat.
- Mix the chowder every few minutes when it's reducing, so it doesn't stick or start to burn on the bottom of the pan.

3

- Smooth the Chowder with an emersion blender or regular blender to transform it into a dipping sauce.

If you want, add more grated cheese after it's blended – there's no harm or shame in that!

4

- Slice the chicken breasts into 1 in. pieces lengthwise and set aside while you put together the coating.

5

In a large wide bowl or on a large plate mix the following together:

- 1 C. Panko breadcrumbs
- ¼ C. Grated Parmesan Cheese
- 1 tsp. Granulated Garlic
- 1 tsp. Onion Powder
- A sprinkle of Cayenne if you like spice
- 1 tsp. of Salt
- ½ tsp. of Black Pepper

This is the simplest way to make baked chicken fingers, in my opinion. They always turn out crunchy & the chicken is very moist – never dry.

6
- Press the chicken fingers into the breadcrumb spice mixture on all sides. This is a thin coating method – more chicken, less coating.

7
- Place the fingers on a foil lined sheet pan and sprinkle with olive oil or any oil of your choice.
- I also sprinkle the chicken with some dill for extra flavor. If you have cooking spray, you can use that.
- It is essential that the chicken has at least a tiny bit of oil on top to help it brown – the grated cheese in the coating will assist with browning as well.

I know how easy it is to buy chicken fingers from the frozen food section, but I'm telling you, these don't take much at all to prepare & you'll feel better knowing exactly what you & your family are eating – quality food!

Chicken Prep & Fries next.

QUICK & DIRTY ON FRIES:

1 Make your own baked fries by cutting Yukon gold potatoes into ¼ in. slices.

2 Put them in a bowl of cold water, drain the potatoes from the water once you have them all cut.

3 Dry the potatoes on a dish towel or paper towels.

4 Drizzle a couple Tbsp. of oil on the potatoes in a dry bowl so they don't oxidize.

5 Generously salt and pepper the potatoes and toss around for even distribution of flavor.

6
- Line a sheet pan with foil and pour the seasoned raw fries onto the pan.
- These will need to bake at 400 for about **30 minutes**. Check after **25 minutes**. If they are getting golden brown already, take them out.

NOTE: You can try to toss & turn the fries halfway through, but I find when they are only halfway done, they won't release easily from the pan & tend to break.

- The fries come out just as good extra golden brown on 1 side only – believe me!

THEIR DONE!

OR you can take the safe and easy route and do this...
Buy frozen fries and cook them to the package instructions.

EITHER WAY, THIS IS A SPEEDY, TASTY, FUN FOOD DINNER.

QUESO CHOWDER CHICKEN CHOPPED SALAD WITH QUESADILLA CROUTONS

There's nothing wrong with topping your salad with some

Queso Chowder Quesadilla Croutons!

STEPS

1

- Warm 1 C. of the Chowder in a saucepan & render it down on low. You want it on the thick side, so it doesn't make the tortilla soggy. It will take about **15 – 20 minutes**.

2

- Once it looks like it's cooked down about half, turn the burner off and let it set up for **a couple minutes.** It should thicken to the perfect consistency.
- This is a good time to cut up the veggies.

3

- Any type of greens you prefer, is great here. In this particular dish, I used mostly iceberg lettuce with a little romaine.

I think the underused iceberg is great for this since the quesadilla croutons are on the heavier side. Iceberg holds up to the cheesy quesadilla croutons.

- For the dressing, use whatever you want or have on hand. I like to use a mixture of crème & Pico or jarred salsa - just mix them together. It goes very well with the spices from the Queso Chowder.

4

CRÈME

- I've said it before, but to make a quick crème, mix 1 C. Greek yogurt or sour cream & the juice of 1 fresh lime.
- Finish it with a pinch of salt and pepper.
- If it's too thick, put in a splash of water or good chicken stock.

PICO

- To make your own Pico, cut up fresh tomatoes, onions & 1 jalapeno all in a very small dice.
- Dress it with some fresh lime juice, salt, pepper & a sprinkling of cilantro.
- Most stores these days have Pico packaged and ready in the produce section, so if that works best for you, go for it – nobody will know.

- For 4 – Salads, you only need to make 2 large or 4 small Quesadillas. That means you'll need 4 large/8 small tortillas.

5

- To blister your flour tortillas, put them over the flame using thongs if you have a gas stove. It will take about **5 seconds** per side until they start to brown and blister.
- If you have an electric stove, put the tortillas in a large pan on high heat (no fat needed), until they start to brown and puff a little – **10 seconds** a side should do the job.

6

- Toss your greens with dressing in a large bowl and set aside until the quesadillas are finished.

Now onto cheese...Can't have a quesadilla without it, right?

7

- Slice or grate about 1 lb. Cheese - sharp cheddar, provolone, mozzarella or any combination of cheeses you like. You don't need that much due to the reduced Queso Chowder.
- Hey, if you want, use the already grated cheese from the store.

8

- Lay your blistered tortillas onto a large foil lined sheet pan and put on a layer of cheese – just to cover.

9

- After the cheese, dollop with the reduced Chowder & put another layer of cheese on top. The cheese on both sides glues it all together.

10

- Put in the oven on 400 for about **8 - 12 minutes**, or until the cheese starts to melt & ooze out the sides. Once they're done, take the quesadillas off the sheet pan.
- Let them rest a couple minutes for all the ingredients to setup. Otherwise, the cheese and Chowder will all run out. Cut them into bite size pieces.

Look What You Have Now - Quesadilla Croutons.

HOW EASY AND GREAT IS THIS DISH? YOU GET BOTH A SALAD AND A QUESADILLA.

I DON'T KNOW ABOUT YOU, BUT THATS A MATCH MADE IN HEAVEN FOR ME!

TURKEY BURGER CHOWDER

IF YOU'VE MADE CHEESEBURGER CHOWDER, THIS RECIPE IS QUITE SIMILAR.

NIGHT OFF ANGUS
ITS
TURKEY BURGER NIGHT!

STEPS

1
- As with all Chowders, begin by sautéing the bacon in your cast iron or heavy bottomed pot.

2
- When the bacon has rendered out most of it's fat, remove it using thongs and place on paper towels. Chop the bacon into bite size pieces.

3
- To the same pot, add in 3 lbs. Ground Turkey. I steer away from white meat here. Dark turkey meat or a blend is best for this Chowder.
- Using a plastic spatula or spoon, break up the meat on medium low until it's golden brown and cooked through.

4
- Once the meat is done, remove it from the pot & put it aside – just as you did with the bacon.
- Set aside until the **JUICY POTATOES** are complete.

The warm HUG from Chowders – JUICY POTATOES.

5
- I know there is some bacon & beef fat in the pot but add 1 Tbsp. olive oil as well.
- **Trust me!** Due to all the starch in potatoes, they will easily stick to the bottom of your pot.
- Adding splashes of chicken stock while the potatoes & onions cook down will prevent sticking as well.
- To your pot, on medium low heat, add the potatoes, onions, herbs, garlic, salt & pepper.
- If you'd like, add a couple Tbsp. of butter for flavor. **This is optional.** ***See exacts – Page 8.***
- Cook the **JUICY POTATOES** down until the potatoes begin to give off their starch & are tender-crisp. This takes about **10 minutes**.

We're not looking for mashed potatoes. They will continue to cook once all the ingredients are together in the pot.

Here's the Secret. Turkey YES. But what makes this Chowder stand on its OWN is...

AVOCADO & SOUR CREAM

6

- To the tender-crisp, creamy **JUICY POTATOES**, it's time to dump all the goodness into the pot: Bacon, browned ground turkey, carrots, celery – season with salt & pepper & add the stock.

Note – Seasoning with salt & pepper every time you add an ingredient, will result in a much tastier & well-rounded flavor

7

- Put a lid onto the pot (ajar) and cook on medium low for approximately **45 minutes** to an hour.
- Check to be sure that it's not bubbling too much, you're looking for a light simmer. If it bubbles too much, you can easily burn yourself & also make a mess of your stove.
- After **45 minutes**, taste for seasoning & texture. If it's still on the thin side, take the lid off and cook for another **10 - 15 minutes**.

8

- This is where the Secret emerges: 2 Avocados (mashed) & ½ C. Sour Cream.
- Stir everything together over low heat, along with the Half & Half or Heavy Cream.

ARGUABLY- THIS TURKEY BURGER IN A BOWL IS A SERIOIUS RIVAL TO IT'S COUNTERPOINT CHEESEBURGER CHOWDER.

The 2 secret ingredients just might take it over the edge!

TURKEY BURGER *Shake Ups*

1. Turkey Burger Flour Tostadas
2. Turkey Burger Stuffed Potatoes
3. Turkey Meat Sauce with Penne

TURKEY BURGER FLOUR TOSTADAS

GUIDE FOR TOSTADAS

STEPS

1
- **Preheat your oven to 400**.
- Warm the strained Chowder – in a small saucepan on medium low heat, until some of the jus has evaporated. It will only take about **5 minutes**.

2
- While that's happening, brush/rub olive oil on flour tortillas & place them in the oven on foil once the oven has come to temp.
- The tortillas will only take **5 -7 minutes**.
- They are going back into the oven once you top them with Chowder & cheese.

Speaking of that, let's do it...

3
- Layer the reduced Chowder onto the crisp tortilla.

4
- Top the Chowder with grated cheese of your choice (Cheddar, Fontina, Monterey Jack, Gouda, etc.), put it back in the oven on a baking sheet for **7 - 10 minutes**.
- The timing in the oven depends upon the thickness of your Chowder & Cheese layers.

Nobody's Judging!

TURKEY BURGER STUFFED POTATOES

There are Two great features in this SHAKE-UP.

POTATOES from Turkey Burger Chowder **(JUICY POTATOES).**
POTATOES Stuffed with Turkey Burger Chowder

Here's your new "Turkey Burger & Fries" Shake-Up.

STEPS

1
- **Preheat your oven to 400**.
- For 4 - 6 Servings, roast 4 - 6 large Russet Potatoes for 1 hour on a foil lined sheet pan.
- Extra-large appetites will be satisfied with 1 whole stuffed potato/2 halves.
- Smaller portion eaters will be more than happy with 1 half Chowder Stuffed Potato.

2
- Reduce 1 C. Chowder in a small saucepan on medium low.
- If it bubbles too much, turn it down to low.
- For topping the stuffed potatoes, while the potatoes are roasting, sear about 6 pieces of bacon - if you want.

3
- After **1 hour**, take the potatoes out of the oven & let rest for **10 minutes**.

4
- Cut the potatoes in half length-wise.
- Into s large bowl, scoop out the "meat" of the potato being sure to leave at least 1 in. of potato on the skin. Your outside layer/potato skins need to be thick enough to hold up to the stuffing.

5
To the bowl of potato stuffing add:
- Your reduced Chowder
- 1 C. Sour Cream
- 4 Tbsp. Room Temp/softened Butter
- 1 C. Grated Cheddar Cheese

6
- Using a handheld masher or mixer, mix everything together with a couple pinches of salt & pepper.

7 Spoon the stuffing into each of your potato skins, top with some more grated cheese (1 C.) & place them back into the oven for another **15 minutes** or until the cheese is melted. Feel free to top with some bacon pieces, chives or scallions if you wish.

THESE ARE NOT YOUR HAND HELD PICK UP STUFFED POTATOES.

A knife, fork & many napkins are necessary!

TURKEY MEAT SAUCE WITH PENNE

Another go-to Shake-Up on a crazy busy day, or for that matter, a lazy day.

STEPS

1
- In a large saucepan (3 QT. for 4 servings or 6 QT. for 6 to 8 servings), heat a couple cups of Chowder.

2
- To the Chowder, add 1 C. of your favorite store bought or homemade marinara and stir together until combined.
- Check for seasoning.

If you and your family are marinara fans, feel free to add an additional cup.
****As you can see, I added sliced mushrooms to increase body to the dish.***
With or without, this Shake-Up will bring you home.

3
- Add your dried Penne pasta to the same saucepan with the Chowder and marinara sauce. I know this is unconventional, but believe me, it works. It's called the 'Risotto' method.
- **Risotto method is simple** – Stir the pasta every few minutes & the starch adds creaminess. Also, without having to boil a large pot of water, it takes steps off your plate. And – **LESS DISHES TO WASH**.
- If you are feeding 4 people, 1 lb. of penne is perfect. Should you be cooking 6 - 8 portions, 2 lb. of penne is keeping it on the safe side, incase somebody wants seconds or thirds.
- Add more stock from the Chowder or just boxed chicken stock if you need more liquid for the pasta. It should only take **7 – 8 minutes** for the pasta to be cooked to al dente.
- Plate the pasta dish (or put it in a bowl), and top with some grated Parmesan or Pecorino cheese.
- Basil or parsley are a great topper as well. It tastes and looks pretty.

TURKEY BURGER CHOWDER TRANSFORMED INTO: MEAT SAUCE WITH PENNE

PRESTO! A beautiful blushed meat sauce and pasta dinner.

CHILI CHOWDER

Chili with those warming spices we all know,
but with the comfort of a Hearty Chowder.

STEPS

Go ahead & add some beans if you'd like. This is how easy it goes...

1
- Make the bacon, take it out of the pot & chop it into bite size pieces.

2
- In the same pot, put in your room temp ground meat.
- 2 lb. Beef, Turkey, Chicken or any combination is yummy in this Chowder

3
Season the meat with the following:
- 1 Tbsp. salt
- ½ Tbsp. pepper
- 2 tsp. Onion powder
- 2 tsp. Granulated garlic – or powder
- 2 Tbsp. Chili Powder
- 2 Tbsp. Cumin
- 2 Tbsp. Coriander
- 2 tsp. Dried Oregano
- ½ tsp. Chili flake – more if you're a spicy one.

4
- Sauté the meat & spices together until your meat has broken up & you can smell the spices bloom.

5
- Remove the meat to rest with your bacon while you make the **JUICY POTATOES (Pg. 8)** & sauté the **veg/DNA (Pg. 5)**.
- It only takes **5 minutes** for the veg to begin cooking. Everything will continue to cook in the Chowder.

6
- Return the chopped bacon & spiced meat.

7
- Add in 2 – 3 Qt. Chicken or Beef stock & a 28 Oz. can of tomatoes. I prefer whole San Marzano's. Break them up with a wooden spoon, a potato masher or better yet, your hands.
- Put a lid on ajar & simmer on medium low heat for **45 minutes** – stirring every few minutes so that the starch in potatoes doesn't stick to the bottom of the pot.

8
- After **45 minutes**, take the lid off & taste for seasoning & texture.
- Should it not be thick enough for you, let it simmer for another **15 minutes** or until you're happy with it.

9
- Incorporate ½ C. Half & Half or Heavy Cream off the heat, so that it doesn't curdle.

BRING IT HOME, OR SHOULD I SAY, KEEP IT AT HOME.
WHEN YOU HAVE THIS CHOWDER ON YOUR LAP,
DON'T BOTHER GOING OUT!

CHILI *Shake Ups*

1. Chili Frittata

2. Chili Rice Bowl

3. Chili Pasta with Peas

CHILI FRITTATA

This Shake-Up IS PERFECT for brunch, lunch, dinner. BETTER YET, a casual cocktail party as you can eat this hot, warm, or room temperature

BELIEVE IN CHILI & EGGS. THEY BELONG TOGETHER!

STEPS

Ok, I'll admit it's feeling a bit like Groundhog Day when starting Shake-Ups by reducing your Chowder on low for about 10 minutes in a saucepan.
But hey, you have a better chance of remembering it, right?

1

- For this Frittata, reduce 1 C. Chili Chowder.
- The Chowder needs to thicken just a bit, so it doesn't water down the eggs.
- **Preheat your oven to 450**.

2

- Speaking of eggs, using a whisk, whip the eggs in a large bowl until you see small bubbles form.
- It makes for a light pillowy Frittata.
- If you've made a Frittata before, the recipe most likely called for some heavy cream
- to be added while whipping the eggs.
- In this case, there is no need to add any cream as the Chili Chowder will incorporate creaminess to the dish.
- You also don't need to add salt or pepper to the eggs due to all the flavors in the Chowder.

This recipe is about to get very complicated so brace yourself.

3

- Mix your reduced Chowder into the whisked eggs.

4

- Pour it all into an ovenproof nonstick skillet rubbed with some butter.

***Note - Feel free to top the eggs with some grated cheese. I do. There's never anything wrong with eggs & cheese!**

- Place the skillet in your **450 oven** & wait all of **10 – 12 minutes**.

YOU'LL KNOW ITS DONE, WHEN YOU WIGGLE THE SKILLET & THE EGGS ARE JUST SET

USE A FORK IF YOU WANT, BUT THIS DISH CAN EASILY BE EATEN AS FINGER FOOD.

EITHER WAY, IT WILL NOT STICK AROUND VERY LONG.
DOUBLING THE RECIPE IS A GOOD IDEA.
WHEN YOU'RE RUNNING OUT THE DOOR OR JUST HAVE A TON GOING ON, A SLICE OF THIS FRITTATA WILL KEEP UP YOUR ENERGY.

THINK OF IT AS A SUGAR FREE ENERGY BAR.
SO GOOD FOR YOU!

CHOWDER & EGGS LOOKING QUITE COZY.
THIS ISN'T THE 1ST DATE OR THE 2ND.
IT LOOKS MUCH MORE LIKE THE 3RD DATE, DOESN'T IT?

CHILI RICE BOWL

There are a total of 4 steps in this SHAKE-UP. None of which take much effort or time.

STEPS

1 Warm ½ C. of your Chowder in a saucepan on low for **10 minutes**.

2 Make 1 C. long grain rice (Jasmine or Basmati) to package directions, minus **2 minutes**, so it doesn't get soggy in the finished rice bowl. I prefer stock over water for flavor, but that's your call.

3 In a large skillet or wok, if you own one, heat some (1 - 2 Tbsp.) clear oil (sunflower, safflower, vegetable, grapeseed) on very high.

4 Put everything together in the hot skillet – reduced Chowder & rice. Stir-fry it quickly for a max of **2 minutes** (with some frozen peas if you'd like). As you can see, I do. Texture & a little sweetness in this dish doesn't hurt. Plus, it's easy on the eyes. You eat with your eyes first.

If I was home alone, I'd be eating this straight away out of the pan

Should you want to put some lipstick on it, give it a plate or bowl.

EVERYONE'S INTO RICE BOWLS.

Shake It Up & TRY THIS VERSION.

CHILI PASTA

STEPS

1 Warm that yummy Chowder on low for approximately **10 minutes**.

2 Throw in a couple handfuls of frozen cauliflower (or chopped fresh) – about ½ C. or more if you love cauliflower.
Sweet cauliflower & peas together with zesty Chowder & pasta is a darn good combination.

3 Toss in about ¼ C. of frozen peas to round out all the flavors.
If you use whole wheat pasta, it can be considered a roll in the hay. *See below ;)
I used Penne in this dish. I think with the Chowder & veg, a short pasta turns out well – nothing wrong with a long pasta either.

ROLL – PEAS, WHEAT PASTA – HEY, CHOWDER – FIERY. THE CAULIFLOWER COMES ALONG FOR THE RIDE.

What a fantastic date night!

CLAM CHOWDER

There will not be any ***Shake-Ups*** with this Chowder.

IT DESERVES THE RESPECT TO STAND ON ITS OWN.

STEPS

1
- Since there isn't any other meat in this Chowder, just render down your bacon (remove & chop into bite size pieces) & move onto the...**JUICY POTATOES!**
- I know the recipe is throughout this book, but I'm delighted to reiterate it again...

2
- Begin with 1 large onion to every 2 large Russet potatoes.
- 1 onion & 2 potatoes are enough for 6 - 8 portions. Should you be making enough for a large family or group, double it.

3
- Chop the onions into a medium dice and slice the potatoes into about ¼ in. slices.

4
- **Add**: 1 tsp. salt
- ½ tsp. pepper
- 1 tsp. Thyme - fresh or dried
- 1 tsp. Rosemary - fresh (finely diced)
- 2 Bay leaves

5
- Sauté everything in a skillet on medium heat with a combination of & olive oil & butter (optional).
- For 6 - 8 portions, 2 Tbsp. of olive oil & the same amount of butter are spot on.
- Again, butter is optional, but WOW, does it take it over the top.
- Be sure to splash in some chicken stock or water as the onions & potatoes are cooking to keep the starchy potatoes from sticking to the pot.

6
- Once the onions are translucent and the potatoes are tender (but not overcooked), they are ready for the remaining base of all your Chowders - next.
- **JUICY POTATOES** will take a total of about **15 minutes** from start to finish.

Now, onto the rest of the DNA & Clams.

7
- Drop in your chopped carrots, celery, grated garlic & season with salt & pepper.

8 After they sauté for about **5 minutes** in the pot of **JUICY POTATOES**, your chopped bacon returns.

9 It's time to add the canned clams & clam juice – see amounts below.

TIPS

- I like to add fresh littleneck clams as well, but you certainly don't have to – especially if cost & ease of finding might be a problem.
- *Should you incorporate fresh clams - **BURP THEM**.*
- *What that means is simply putting them in a large bowl of cold H2O. They will spit out the sand inside.*

CRUNCHY SANDY CHOWDER – NO THANKS!

- Also, remember to not incorporate until the VERY end – right when you are ready to serve. They only need about **5 minutes** to cook. You'll know they're done when they pop open.
- If they don't open, **DO NOT** eat them – **DISREGARD**.
- That means they are long gone. Nobody should be eating those!

All in all, the Chowder really is just as delicious without fresh clams.

10 **ADD:** Three 10 oz. cans of whole shelled baby clams. Three 8 oz. bottles of clam juice from your grocery.

If you are making closer to 8 servings, some additional stock might be needed. Chicken stock works fine, but you can, of course, use seafood stock. The amount you add depends on how thick or thin you want your Chowder. Be gentile. It's best to play on the thicker side & add as you need

11 Cook the Chowder on medium low until the **JUICY POTATOES** have played its part.
It has thickened & pulled everything together. This should take maybe **30 minutes**.
The flavor is intense, so it doesn't require a long cooking time.
As I always say, check for seasoning – salt & pepper.

Taste taste taste! There isn't any other way to know the quality of your dish. You didn't put the time & energy into this Chowder to serve it mediocre style!

12 After **30 minutes** of cooking down...Off the heat, add 1 C. cream or half & half.
Squeezing in some fresh lemon juice at the very end for brightness, brings it home.

CHOWDER MAKES EVERYBODY HAPPY. TIME FOR YOU & YOURS TO ENJOY A BEAUTIFUL BOWL OF COMFORTING CLAM CHOWDER.

Now get in the kitchen & Shake-Up life through food!

INDEX

Milton Keynes UK
Ingram Content Group UK Ltd.
UKHW051549181023
430817UK00004B/20

* 9 7 8 1 0 8 8 0 8 9 1 0 1 *